Robert Guthrie · The PKU Story

Also by Jean Holt Koch

Understanding the Mentally Retarded Child: A New Approach
with Richard Koch, M.D.

ROBERT GUTHRIE

THE PKU STORY

A CRUSADE AGAINST
MENTAL RETARDATION

By Jean Holt Koch

Hope Publishing House, Pasadena, California

For information address:

Hope Publishing House
P.O. Box 60008
Pasadena, CA 91116 – U.S.A.
Tel: 818-792-6123, Fax: 818-792-2121
E-mail: hopepub@loop.com / http://www.hope-pub.com

Design and composition by Greg Endries
Printed in the U.S.A. on acid-free paper

Library of Congress Cataloging-in-Publication Data

Koch, Jean.
 Robert Guthrie — the PKU story : crusade against mental retardation /
by Jean Holt Koch.
  p. cm.
 Include bibliographical references and index.
 ISBN 0-932727-91-3
 1. Guthrie, Robert, 1916–1995. 2. Physicians — United States —
Biography. 3. Medical scientists — United States — Biography.
4. Phenylketonuria — Diagnosis. 5. Mental retardation — Prevention.
6. Medical screening. 7. Infants (Newborn) — Diseases — Diagnosis.
 I. Title.
 [DNLM: 1. Guthrie, Robert. 1916–1995. 2. Physicians — biography. 3. Phenylketonuria — epidemiology. 4. Neonatal Screening. WZ
100 G9838K 1997]
R154.G827K63 1997
610'.92-dc21
[B]
DNLM/DLC
for Library of Congress   97-2457
                 CIP

Contents

This book is dedicated to the memory of

JOHN GUTHRIE,

Robert and Margaret Guthrie's son, who died peacefully in his sleep February 7, 1995. His wry sense of humor brought laughter to many. His sense of morality was strong. His life led family and friends to a greater understanding of the challenges faced by persons with mental handicaps. Because of John Guthrie several members of his family have dedicated themselves to the cause of helping those with mental handicaps. John's birth inspired his father, Bob Guthrie, to work untiringly to prevent mental retardation worldwide.

Acknowledgments

I am indebted to many people who helped me prepare this manuscript. The first, of course, is Bob Guthrie, who furnished me with accounts of his many travels—including tapes and snapshots. During long hours of interviews he patiently defined liver fractions and explained laboratory procedures so this layperson could understand how a bacterial inhibition assay works. Beyond this, he recommended that I join the computer age when my ancient typewriter gave up the ghost.

My thanks also go to Bob's wife, Margaret, and to their children—Anne, Barbara, Jim, Patty and Tom—who all shared with me their memories of life in the Guthrie household. Anne's husband Richard Gaeta, a good friend to John Guthrie, gave me a deeper insight into Johnnie, and for this I owe him my thanks. Also my appreciation goes to Sally Bloom, Bob's program coördinator, who was indispensable to his success, and to Dr. Louis Woolf, who related firsthand the story of the development of the first phenylalanine restricted formula. Others who helped me unravel the story include Joan Edwards, Sally's eventual successor who now administers the Developmental Disabilities Prevention Program in Williamsville, New York, and Kathi Hilbert, Bob's secretary who transcribed hundreds of pages of notes for this manuscript.

Dr. Willard Centerwall provided much of the material about Dr. Fölling's discovery of PKU. He was responsible for the fact that Pinky was diagnosed and treated from birth for PKU, making her story come alive.

I thank Dr. Neil Buist for an enlightening lecture on hydrolysates which helped pass the time aboard an airplane over the Atlantic

Ocean, and Dr. Imdad Sardharwalla, who provided statistics on iodine deficiency diseases. I appreciate Dr. Kenneth A. Pass for allowing the use of his article on newborn screening for sickle cell disease. And I am grateful to those who were interviewed for this book—Mary Lou Doll, the mother of Bob's niece Margaret; Mr. and Mrs. Higgins, parents of David and Kathy; Nickelle W. and her mother; the mother of Susan; and to Donna Triglio.

I am especially indebted to the following, without whose aid this publication would not be possible: Bob Phillips, inventor of the punch index machine that automated the Guthrie test; the Monsanto Company; Mark DeFries, chief executive officer of S.H.S. America; Bryan Gill, managing director of S.H.S. International; Ross Products Division, Abbott Laboratories; the Mead Johnson Nutritional Company; Schleicher and Schuell, Inc. and People Inc.

My appreciation goes to others who have read this manuscript and given me moral support in its completion: Dr. Gunnar Dybwad; Peter Leibert, Prevention Chair of the Association for Retarded Citizens; Dr. Joseph Ireland for his thorough editing and his input on the beginnings of PKU screening in England; Dr. Georgirene Vladutiu; and Denise Sherwood, who helped me unravel some of the mysteries of my computer. Lastly I thank my husband, Dr. Richard Koch, who proof-read and advised, was my consultant on medical matters and who gave me my computer. I couldn't have done it without any of you.

— JEAN HOLT KOCH

Preface

Robert Guthrie was a remarkable man and Jean Koch has rendered the world a service in writing this account of his life. Guthrie's name will always be linked to phenylketonuria (PKU), the disease he did so much to conquer. PKU is a devastating condition producing profound mental retardation, behavioral abnormalities and, often, epilepsy as described so well by Jean Koch in her accounts of Margaret Doll, Kathy H. and David H. Affected children posed an almost insupportable problem for their parents and other family members—"posed" in the past tense partly because of the work of Bob Guthrie.

In 1951 the theory was put forward that the clinical features of PKU were the result of a toxic action by phenylalanine, a component of all proteins and protein-containing foods. Treatment with a diet containing very little phenylalanine was suggested. In 1953 Horst Bickel, John Gerrard and Evelyn Hickmans published the first report of amelioration of the mental retardation and behavioral abnormalities by such treatment. The account Jean Koch gives of Nickelle W., Pinky, and Susan M. are typical of the propitious effect of a phenylalanine-restricted diet—in marked contrast to Margaret Doll, Kathy H. and David H., who were untreated or treated too late.

In 1955 it was pointed out that for optimum effect the phenylalanine–restricted diet should be started before three weeks of age, long before there were any clinically detectable signs of PKU. This would necessitate testing the urine of apparently well infants, using ferric chloride (at that time the only simple test for PKU). Logically this led to the need to test the urine of all newborn infants. Despite initial objections that such a proposal was impractical if not downright crazy, many pediatricians and public health physicians—who are naturally the most keenly aware of the difficulty of treating mental retardation effectively once it has become established—accepted the idea of trying to prevent the condition. Programs to test the urine of all newborn infants in Los Angeles (by Willard and Siegried Centerwall) and in Cardiff, Wales, were started. There were many practical difficulties in obtaining and testing the urine. Although improved urine tests were introduced, the testing of blood proved simpler and more reliable.

Bob Guthrie made three major contributions to newborn screening programs, any one of which would have earned him a place of honor in the history of the fight against mental retardation. He showed that it was simple and safe to obtain blood specimens as spots on filter paper—the famous "Guthrie cards." He developed the bacterial inhibition assay for phenylalanine in the blood spot, the first method of diagnosing PKU on a population basis using blood. Most importantly he proselytized tirelessly all over the world for the early detection of PKU and other conditions which can lead to mental retardation if they remain untreated. It is due to this evangelism that newborn screening is now routinely carried out in all developed and many developing countries of the world. As Jean Koch says in her book, Bob Guthrie was an excellent salesperson.

The central feature of the Guthrie test is the use of blood spots on thick filter paper which also bears a written or printed record identifying the infant. The blood is usually obtained by a heel prick a few days after birth since it takes a little time for the concentration of phenylalanine in the blood to build up. In the early days of population screening a few infants with PKU were not picked up because the blood had been collected too soon after birth. Jean Koch gives a fascinating account of the steps in the evolution of this method of obtaining a specimen for the laboratory as well as of the bacterial inhibition assay. Despite his training as a bacteriologist, Bob

Guthrie was not indissolubly wedded to the bacterial inhibition assay. He repeatedly said he would be perfectly happy to see the blood spots used for paper chromatography, fluorimetric assay or any other reliable test for PKU. As Jean Koch points out, the blood spots are now used for testing many other conditions besides PKU and various techniques such as radio-immuno assay for detecting hypothyroidism are used. Neonatal hypothyroidism in North America is twice as common as PKU and, if not treated promptly after birth, just as devastating to the affected individual and that person's family. As with PKU, by the time clinical signs of the disease are detectable, it is too late for fully effective treatment.

Like all pioneers Bob Guthrie met with his measure of disbelief and opposition. But he refused to be deterred. Nor did he allow mere convention to hamper him in doing what he knew was right. When he had difficulty in getting his work accepted by a leading journal, he published in the local newspaper and sent cuttings all over the world. It was this crusading spirit in overcoming obstacles that was his outstanding characteristic and led to the present programs throughout the world to prevent mental retardation.

Jean Koch's book paints a picture of the man as a whole, not just the scientist. This is perhaps the book's chief merit, for it highlights that scientists are people with the same family commitments, problems, successes, failures, hobbies as everyone else—and these interact with their scientific work. We shall never know to what extent Bob Guthrie's devotion to the prevention of mental retardation was due to his son John's retardation. It is doubtful Bob himself knew. What is certain, though, is that because of his efforts many individuals have been saved from a life spent in institutions for those with mental retardation. This book is a worthy monument in honor of a man to whom the world owes much.

—L.I. Woolf
Vancouver

Foreword

When I was asked if I would write a biography of Robert Guthrie, I was delighted. Bob Guthrie was a personal friend who grew in my esteem the longer I knew him. My husband, Dr. Richard Koch, was a deputy director of California's health department in 1975 when he hired Bob Guthrie as a part-time consultant. Bob was the famous doctor who had developed the screening test for PKU and who had traveled extensively, touching the lives of thousands of people in his crusade to prevent mental retardation. Bob was to spend every other month in California, studying and advising on matters of prevention. I was asked if Bob could use our spare room during his stays in Sacramento. At first I was intimidated at the prospect of having such a prestigious houseguest, but I need not have worried.

Bob turned out to be a soft-spoken, gentle man who easily became a part of our family. He was a caring person, who never complained unless I served meat or fish for dinner. Even then, he did not complain, but simply satisfied himself with whatever else I served, as he would not eat anything that had been a living creature. He had a ready sense of humor and loved social occasions. But he was deeply serious about the need to follow through on all programs that would prevent mental retardation. When he felt some action was necessary, he was unrelenting. And sometimes he stepped on the wrong toes. But his dedication had to be admired.

Bob endured my cooking, a standard-size bed that was perhaps a little short for his six-foot frame, and my haircuts when he became shaggy. He became a welcome guest and he, Dick and I spent many evenings discussing the events of the day over glasses of California wine.

Introduction

Dylan James Guthrie was born on July 26, 1991, at Lawrence Memorial Hospital in Lawrence, Kansas. Before he left the hospital, a few drops of blood were taken from his heel and put on a special filter paper and mailed, along with one from each newborn infant at the hospital, to a laboratory in Topeka where special tests were done. Often new parents do not even notice the small addition to their hospital bill for this procedure, and if they do, they do not understand the purpose. But the parents of Dylan James Guthrie understood everything perfectly, and were so interested, they even videotaped the whole procedure.

The aim of these tests is to determine whether an infant who appears to be normal at birth has one of a number of disorders that can cause severe disabilities or death if not treated early. This procedure is known as neonatal screening and is a growing practice making it possible to begin early treatment of these disorders that some years ago were unheard of and untreatable.

In addition, such specimens are collected from all infants born in every industrialized country in the world as well as in many developing nations, in South America and many regions of China. Why is this so and how did it come about? It is the purpose of this book to answer these questions as well as to describe other types of preventive techniques that can save many infants and children from the effects of serious disorders. Another aim of this book is to tell the story of Dylan's grandfather, Robert Guthrie, who developed the technique and dedicated his professional life to the prevention of illness in children all over the world.

Robert Guthrie, M.D., Ph.D., (1916–1995)

Evolution of an Evangelist

When PKU (phenylketonuria) was first described as a medical disorder by Dr. Asbjörn Fölling in 1934, no one could have realized the impact his discovery would have in the field of medicine. Among those whose lives would never be the same was an 18 year-old high school student in Minneapolis, Minnesota. That young student thought he might like to become a writer or maybe a chemical engineer, but he did not have the money or the grade-point average to attend college at that time. His name was Robert Guthrie. The son of a traveling salesman, he was to become known throughout the world as the larger-than-life person who developed the newborn screening test for PKU and it was in his laboratory that tests for some 30 other disorders were developed. Bob Guthrie devoted his professional career to the prevention of mental retardation.

Bob's interests were not limited to the field of PKU. Years before most members of the medical profession became concerned about lead poisoning, Bob Guthrie was aware and was waging a battle to educate his colleagues and the public about this insidious peril.

Bob was a crusader for other causes. He worked to improve race relations. He campaigned for improvements in the public schools in his community. He was a member of Physicians for Social Responsibility, a respected organization of doctors who know the dreadful consequences of nuclear war and actively oppose nuclear weapons testing.

Although Bob Guthrie's phenomenal development of a simple, inexpensive method of diagnosing treatable disorders in newborns has saved untold numbers of children from mental retardation, he was never able to find the cause of mental retardation in his own son John. According to Bob, his son's disability made him acutely aware of the problems faced by many people with disabilities and their families. It was a stimulus for him to strive unceasingly for the development of new methods for the prevention of mental retardation.

These opening paragraphs have been written after the rest of the book was completed and with deep sadness. On June 24, 1995, the world lost Bob Guthrie. He would have been 79 years old in a few days. His loss will be felt keenly by his friends and colleagues.

Bob Guthrie was a humble man. But he was a giant in the field of medicine.

This is his story.

Robert Guthrie was born in 1916 in Marionville, Missouri, a small town in the Ozark Mountains. He was the second son of Reginald and Ina Florence Ledbetter Guthrie. His brother Bill was five years older than Bob. Although his family left Marionville before he was two years old, Bob claimed all of his life to be a hillbilly. For several years his father, Reginald Joseph Guthrie, taught school in Marionville. Later he worked as a traveling salesman, first selling Gold Medal Flour and later wholesaling White Sewing Machines to furniture stores. Everybody called him "Joe" except Bob's mother who called him "Reg." The family lived in Lincoln, Nebraska, for three years during Bob's early childhood. However, Joe Guthrie did most of his traveling throughout Minnesota and Wisconsin.

Bob had a variety of jobs while he was growing up. He remembered the first job he held when he was four years old. His brother was selling magazines door-to-door, so young Bob decided to sell magazines, too. Everyone was amazed when he came home with some coins in his pocket and fewer magazines in his inventory. He succeeded early as a salesman.

When Bob was six the family moved to Minneapolis where he spent his school years. He accompanied his father on some of his selling trips during school vacations. A successful salesman even during the worst of the depression, Joe Guthrie traveled in a Model A Ford and always carried a used White Sewing Machine with him just in case he found a buyer. He also checked the classified ads in the local paper for items he could buy and resell on his route. He did so well that by 1935 he was driving a brand new Ford—the fastest car on the road.

Bob learned a lot on those trips with his father about making sales, a skill he later used tirelessly in his campaign to prevent mental retardation. His father would go into a furniture store and greet the owners, always remembering their names. Joe would ask about the family and talk about fishing—a safe subject in Wisconsin as well as Minnesota, a state with 17,000 lakes. He would remember which lakes were nearby and which were favorites of the owners. Even without a card file he seemed to remember everything about his customers. Then when he was ready to leave he would say, "What'll it be this time?" and he would take the orders for sewing machines. That was the only time during the visit that sewing machines were discussed. Joe carried other items with him which he sold as opportunity allowed. Bob recalled one occasion when he and his father entered a barber shop and his father sold some beads to a man sitting in the chair having a shave. Joe Guthrie was an excellent salesman, mainly due to his out-going nature and genuine interest in people.

Another job young Bob held was selling dust mops door-to-door. A company called Dustmasters sponsored a softball team on which he and his brother played. Bill, a natural athlete, was pitcher and Bob played center field. It was the only time Bob ever played baseball. Perhaps one of the incentives was the baseball jacket provided by Dustmasters.

As a child Bob loved science fiction books. He read incessantly, often by flashlight under the covers after he had been sent to bed. He was a "night person" from the start. In grammar school he often missed school classes because his mother, realizing he had not had enough sleep, would write excuses for him. His sixth grade teacher at Richfield Roosevelt School encouraged him to enter a city-wide writing contest in Minneapolis. He won first place with a story about a knight in armor. About that time he decided to become a writer.

Bob attended a number of different schools in Minneapolis because his father never owned a home. He did own a vacation place on Lake Minnetonka where the family spent each summer. The family simply moved out of whatever house they were renting and moved to the lake each summer. Then in the fall Joe would rent another house in Minneapolis and the family would move back to the city. During his summers at the lake Bob learned to paddle canoes and started going on canoe trips with some of his friends. Later he graduated to sailboats and sailing became a lifelong passion. His first sailboat, when he was twelve, was his father's rowboat rigged with a square sail made from a porch curtain. In 1937 he bought a canoe from Montgomery Wards in St. Paul for $67. With a lateen sail his mother made on her sewing machine, he made it a sailing canoe. Hauling the canoe tied to the top of a car, he and his friends took it sailing on many lakes around Minneapolis. That sailing canoe stayed in the family; his son has it now in Kansas.

Robert had an active social life in high school, taking part in plays and assemblies. He even wore a suit and tie to school, something he did later in life only under duress. But he was not a consistent student. He did well in the subjects he liked but did not study for the other classes. In fact, his German teacher kept threatening to fail him so he wouldn't graduate. Bob did find time to help students who needed tutoring in mathematics or other subjects. The city was prepared to pay him for his work but for some reason he never collected the money. In spite of those threats from his German teacher, he did graduate in 1935 without academic distinction, at the top of the lower third of his class of 400 students.

Bob wanted to go to the university but the 1930s were depression years. Although his father was a successful salesman, Bob had to settle for going back to high school as a post-graduate student with a solid curriculum of algebra, trigonometry and solid geometry, shorthand and typing. In addition he enrolled in a chemistry class at night school. Then he heard about the National Youth Administration (NYA), a program begun during the Roosevelt administration in which college students could earn small salaries while enrolled in classes. He applied for admission to the University of Minnesota. He was accepted for the spring semester on the condition that he pass an academic exam to counter his low grade point average from high school.

Under the NYA Bob worked for different faculty members and earned the magnificent sum of $15 a month. This was enough to cover tuition and incidental fees, just $31 per quarter. Bob's family lived three miles from the university so he was able to ride his bicycle to school. His job in a cafeteria provided 88 cents worth of food every day, a welcome supplement to his salary. Later he moved even closer to school by entering into a unique arrangement with the mother of one of his friends who ran a rooming house for students. For 75 cents a week he rented space on a stair landing where he put an army cot.

When Bob made the decision to become a chemical engineer, he dressed the part, sporting a sweatshirt and leather jacket and carrying a slide rule. For the first quarter he excelled academically. He had always been interested in astronomy and had read many books about it. He even considered majoring in astronomy and minoring in microbiology. However his astronomy professor discouraged him saying, "Young man, do you know how many full-time astronomers there are in the United States? There are six of us!"

Another incentive for attending astronomy class was an attractive girl who sat next to him in the front row. There was only one problem: a well-dressed boy sat on his other side and conversed with this lovely girl as if Bob did not exist. However, when the results of the first exam were posted on the wall showing Bob at the top of the class, they began to include him in the conversation.

Margaret Flagstad was another new friend who sat near him in organic chemistry class. She was studying to be a medical technician, taking the required class along with the premedical students. Since Bob was not doing well in the class, he often borrowed her notes. Margaret and Bob both ended up with a D in the class, the only D Margaret ever got. Although they had not done too well in college chemistry, Bob and Margaret experienced a different kind of chemistry and began dating in 1937.

Under the NYA program, Bob worked in the department of bacteriology and immunology where he met Charles, the brother of his old friend John Evans. Charles, having earned an M.D. and a Ph.D., suggested Bob apply for admission to medical school. Bob considered this, although he was uncertain about a career as a doctor. When he mentioned it to a friend who was going to nursing school, she responded, "Oh, you will never be a doctor." He took that as a challenge.

Bob was also moved by the book *Arrowsmith* by Sinclair Lewis which described a research physician who lost track of time because he was so absorbed in his work. Ultimately Bob applied for admission to medical school, certain that he would not be accepted due to a C+ grade point average in his undergraduate work. To his amazement, he was accepted, probably on the basis of oral and written entrance exams at the one medical school where he applied—at the University of Minnesota.

In 1939 Bob started medical school, but he hated it because of the amount of memorization required. He could not imagine anything worse. He especially disliked anatomy, often cutting class in order to attend lectures in quantum mechanics. As a consequence he had to repeat anatomy in the summer when the lab was especially hot and smelly. His experience led him to believe that this was the worst medical school in the world. He discovered later that it was one of the best.

While he was in medical school Bob worked for Dr. Arthur T. Henrici, a professor of microbiology. Bob cared for Dr. Henrici's laboratory animals, usually after the library closed at ten p.m. Dr. Henrici was also a "night owl" and the two of them often talked while Bob cleaned the cages and fed the animals. Dr. Henrici, president of the American Society of Bacteriology, took a special interest in Bob. Knowing Bob did not like medical school, he told him about an opening for a graduate assistant at the University of Maine. Bob applied for the job and was accepted by Dr. Hitchner, head of the department of bacteriology and biochemistry.

In 1940 Bob moved to Orono, Maine, where he felt he had finally found his niche. He was much happier than he had been in medical school. There he met Dr. Stanislaus Sniezko, who turned out to be an influential person in his life. Dr. Sniezko had been the head of the microbiology department at the University of Krakow in Poland. In 1939 when Germany invaded Poland, he and his wife were in the United States at an international meeting on microbiology. After he received asylum in this country, Dr. Sniezko became a faculty member at the University of Maine where Bob served as his assistant in several courses he taught and where they shared a laboratory.

Dr. Sniezko taught Bob how to do flagella stains which led to his choosing an organism as the basis for his master's degree. By a curious coincidence Bob was to discover that the organism he chose was the same organism Dr. Sniezko had been studying in Europe before he came to the United States. *Pseudomonas punctata,* as it is called in Europe, or *Protus hydrophilus,* as it is called in the United States, is a bacterial cell that moves by waving its whip-like arms or flagella. Dr. Sniezko had developed a method of staining the arms of the organism as a form of identification. In Czechoslovakia Dr. Sniezko had found that the bacterium called *Pseudomonas punctata,* an organism with a single arm or flagellum, was causing a disease that was killing the fish in commercial ponds. The solution to the problem in Poland was to control the disease by never mixing the fish from one pond with those of another pond. Dr. Sniezko gave a lecture on this organism to his class at Orono, distributing a relevant handout.

In the meantime Bob had decided to study *Protus hydrophilus* for his master's degree. It was a bacterium that caused a hemorrhagic septicemia or "red belly disease" in frogs in the zoology department of the university. It was thought to be a peritrichous organism or one with many flagella. However, when Bob used the staining technique he had learned from Dr. Sniezko he found that it was a monotrichus organism. While reviewing Dr. Sniezko's handout which had been in his desk for nearly a year, Bob became convinced that the two organisms were the same. Unfortunately the world was embroiled in war and it was impossible at that time to get strains from Europe for comparison. Even so both Dr. Sniezko and Bob agreed that the two organisms were the same—an amazing coincidence!

Years later other scientists recognized the importance of this bacterial species as a widespread pathogen of frogs, fish, turtles and other cold blooded animals living in fresh water. The two organisms were reclassified together as *Aeromonas hydrophila*.

When he returned home for Christmas vacation that year, Bob brought a present for Margaret: a sealed can from the Industrial Microbiology office at the University of Maine. Inside was an engagement ring, purchased with an entire month's salary!

It appeared that the U.S.A. would soon be involved in World War II. Bob received his draft notice, but was classified 4F due to his near-sightedness. Later in the war men like Bob were inducted. However Bob believed that the doctor who examined him felt it was more important for him to finish medical school, a goal he eventually reached.

In 1941 Bob earned his bachelor's degree, completing the requirements taking classes at the University of Maine and by correspondence courses. He also had to have a passing grade for his first year of medical school to qualify for the degree. He made it by one honor point. This qualified him to enter the University of Maine as a graduate student, earning $75 per month as a two-year fellow working for his master's degree in biochemistry.

That fall Robert and Margaret were married and Margaret joined Bob in Orono, Maine. They planned to have two children, never dreaming they would be blessed with six offspring. During this period Margaret was the family breadwinner, working at the State Experimental Station for $100 per month. In addition she earned two dollars each Sunday playing the organ at church.

Although he was working hard to help with expenses, Bob also carried a heavy schedule of classes including chemical thermodynamics (thermo-godam-ics, as the students called it because it was so tough), advanced physical chemistry, hydrophilic physical chemistry, hydrophobic physical chemistry and biochemistry—earning excellent grades. Bob later learned that when he first arrived at the University of Maine Dr. Hitchner was somewhat concerned about him because he never showed up in the morning unless it was absolutely necessary. Actually Bob was continuing his well-established habit of working late every night and sleeping in the next morning. According to Dr. Hitchner, Robert's schedule improved a great deal after he got married.

At the end of his two years at the University of Maine, Bob resisted returning to medical school. He really wanted to earn a Ph.D. in bacteriology instead. In consultation with a number of professionals, Bob was urged and encouraged to finish medical school. Therefore in 1942 Bob and Margaret moved back to Minneapolis where Bob returned to medical school. (Later he often said that the only thing his medical degree did was get his car into the doctors' parking lot at hospitals, but without that medical degree he would not have been able to accomplish all that he achieved in the field of prevention of mental retardation.) But Bob did not give up his dream of getting a Ph.D. He completed the courses for the Ph.D. and took his oral exams at the graduate school—while he was in medical school. It was his private joke that the faculty members at the medical school did not know he was also in graduate school and those at the graduate school did not know he was in medical school.

The University of Minnesota did not grant an M.D. degree until the student had completed one extra year of study on an advanced degree. So Bob spent that year working toward his Ph.D. in bacteriology. His work focused on the nutrition of a protozoan called *Trichomonas fetus* that causes spontaneous abortions in cattle. Bob's supervising professor was Dr. H. Oren Halvorsen who was very interested in bacterial spores. As a result Bob also became interested in spores, an interest that led to the test he later developed for PKU. His thesis for his Ph.D. focused on the nutrition of the *Trichomonas fetus* and Bob spent hours over an old-fashioned microscope counting live protozoa in a cell chamber. Dr. Esmond Snell at the department of agricultural biochemistry at the University of Wisconsin supervised his work.

After earning his M.D. at the University of Minnesota medical school, Bob obtained a prestigious post-doctoral fellowship at the University of Wisconsin working for the National Research Council. This fellowship paid $2,400 per year, which Bob and Margaret thought would be an adequate income for the rest of their lives. During his eleven months in Wisconsin he did all of the research for his Ph.D. thesis and received that degree at the University of Minnesota in August of 1946.

Thus Bob earned six degrees in six years. After his second year in medical school he was able to get a bachelor's degree in science for five dollars which, added to his B.A. and M.A., made three degrees. When he graduated from medical school he earned a bachelor of medicine. After a year of working toward his Ph.D. he earned an M.D. and in 1946 he added the Ph.D. "It was pretty crazy," Bob noted, "but it's just the way it worked out." Never intending to practice medicine, Bob took the licensing exams mainly to satisfy his father, who could not see why anyone would go to medical school if he was not going to practice. In August of 1946 at the age of 30, Bob had an M.D. and a Ph.D. and was ready to begin his career.

Even in the midst of his academic adventure, Bob never gave up his love affair with sailing. During his senior year in medical school he and another student put up $100 each to purchase their first real sailboat—a fast old gaff-rigged class C scow. They could be found on Lake Minnetonka most of that summer. When his partner left, Bob bought his half of the boat from him and sailed it for another year on Lake Nokomis, near Margaret's old home in Minneapolis.

Bob and Margaret's first son, Tom, was born in 1945 in Minneapolis after which the family made their move to Madison, Wisconsin. These years were very busy for Margaret, who was essentially raising their infant son by herself. Fortunately Tom was an easy baby to manage and she was able to cope. But as Bob became increasingly involved in his research and as their family grew the responsibilities of raising the children fell for the most part to Margaret.

During the summer of 1946 Bob was employed at the Argonne Laboratory in Chicago, one of several governmental nuclear energy laboratories around the country that were trying to determine how to measure the radioactivity of carbon-14. Since this was a government nuclear lab, special security clearance was required to work there so Bob applied for clearance. He was finally cleared by the F.B.I.—after he had left the job. That summer Bob would take the train to Chicago every Sunday night, spend the week at the lab and return to Madison on Friday night. He ended up with one souvenir from his job: a radioactive tobacco leaf which he carried in his wallet. A vice president of the Sun Oil Company later asked if he could have the leaf and Bob gave it to him. The leaf became the subject of an article published in the journal *Science*, and Bob got a footnote.

In 1947 Bob went to work as a research microbiologist at the National Institutes of Health in Bethesda, Maryland. This was his first professional position and it was particularly gratifying that an extra bonus came his way each month because he had an M.D. degree in addition to a Ph.D. Soon he was earning the magnificent salary of $4,600 per year. Looking forward to financial security, Bob and Margaret borrowed the down payment for a house from Margaret's father.

Bob assumed that he would continue on a half-time basis doing research on the protozoan *Trichomonas fetus*. He became interested in the work of a bacteriologist from the University of Maryland, Mary Shorb. At a meeting of the Society of American Bacteriology she had presented a paper on *Lactobacillus lactis* Dornier and the growth factor for it, which she had not identified. Bob was intrigued because *Trichomonas fetus* also had an unknown factor, which appeared to be similar to Dr. Shorb's bacterium. Both appeared to be responding to materials that were known to have anti-pernicious anemia factor activity.

Bob's boss was also working on the anti-pernicious anemia factor using a rat assay he had developed. The National Institute of Health had invested heavily in equipment and personnel for a pilot plant to isolate the anti-pernicious anemia factor using the rat assay. As a result there was no interest in *Trichomonas fetus* or Dr. Shorb's work. Subsequently an article appeared in *Science* providing proof that Mary Shorb and some researchers from Merck Laboratories had isolated the anti-pernicious anemia factor. It turned out to be vitamin B-12.

Needless to say, Bob's career did not last long at the NIH once he realized that his boss had no interest in his research on protozoa. In a memo to the head of the department Bob declared that he was going into biochemical genetics and he poured his cultures of protozoa down the sink. Nevertheless Bob's time with the NIH was not wasted. One of his best friends there was Dr. Max Zelle who was working with bacterial viruses in the department of industrial hygiene. Max agreed to teach Bob techniques of bacterial viruses if Bob would teach him biochemistry. Bob doubted that Max benefited much from that bargain. However Bob was able to borrow a sub-stage condenser for phase contrast to count bacterial spores. This was one of the two pieces of phase contrast equipment "liberated" from the Germans by the U.S. Army after World War II. The condenser enabled Bob to count spores, information he later used in his work. He was sure that he could see a darkening of the spores, a characteristic later recognized by him and others as the nuclei in spore-forming bacteria.

There was no way for Bob to know that his decision to go into biochemical genetic research would eventually lead him to "human" biochemical genetics and specifically the discovery of a screening test for newborn infants to detect the disorder, phenylketonuria (PKU). His discovery would enable doctors to begin treatment for those infants affected—before the onset of mental retardation.

After declaring his independence, Bob's future with the NIH did not appear to be very bright. So he accepted an offer to become chair of the department of bacteriology at the University of Kansas starting September 1949. Meanwhile the Guthrie family had grown. In 1947 a second son, John, was born and in 1949, shortly before Bob left the NIH, a daughter, Anne, was born.

Almost immediately problems became apparent at the University of Kansas. Bob's tenure there was even shorter than it had been at the NIH. He was young and naïve, unaware that as many as 30 candidates had refused the position before he had accepted it. He did enjoy working with the graduate students. Following his well-established routine, he often worked in the lab until three a.m.—then joined the graduate students at the Lindiana Cafe for hamburgers. His aim was to get to bed before the children woke up in the morning. During his stressful time at the University of Kansas, Bob succeeded in remodeling some of the laboratories and in doing some of his best research work. He did not publish his work until nearly six years later. He remained in the position for one short year.

Having been head of a department it was difficult for Bob to get an academic position at any level. So he returned to the Public Health Service working at the Staten Island Public Health Hospital supervising the diagnostic bacteriology laboratory. He introduced the use of filter paper discs, each impregnated with a different antibiotic and placed on agar in a petri dish, as a quick way of determining antibiotic sensitivity to a bacterium isolated from a patient. Bob enjoyed his work and liked his boss. Things seemed to be improving for the Guthries. They had purchased a house on Staten Island and Margaret was expecting another baby.

However, after only six months, there was a million-dollar budget cut in the hospital division of the Public Health Service. Bob and many others lost their jobs. The Guthries put the house up for sale and Bob began the search for another position with only ten days of salary remaining. Fortunately he quickly found a position at the Sloan Kettering Institute in Manhattan where he researched the development of better chemotherapeutic agents to treat cancer. Bob and Margaret decided to keep the house and for the next three years Bob commuted by ferry boat from Staten Island to Manhattan. The commute was time-consuming but the ferry ran 24 hours a day allowing Bob to travel back and forth at his own convenience. He was able to adjust his work schedule to his liking, staying overnight at work on Monday, going home late Tuesday night and returning late Wednesday. Then he would stay overnight again Thursday. By sleeping there two nights a week he saved about seven hours of commuting time.

Occasionally a surgical resident would come down from the operating room and find Bob's sleeping form in his bed. Bob thought his plan had hit a snag when Mr. Menke, the administrator, summoned him to his office, but instead of putting an end to his erratic working and sleeping schedule, he gave him a key to much better quarters—the top floor of Ewing Hospital next door to Sloan Kettering. With a pool table, a television and a nice breeze off the East River, the arrangement also afforded him total anonymity. He wore the standard white clothing of the hospital allowing the technicians to think he was a surgeon and the surgeons to think he was a technician. No one knew who he was. It was a great arrangement.

His boss, Dr. Chester Stock, never interfered with Bob's arrangement, which suited him just fine. However one consequence of Bob's extraordinary working schedule was that he sometimes got confused. On at least one occasion, after walking to work, he got a phone call at the Sloan Kettering Institute informing him that he had left his car on the ferry.

At one point the director of Sloan Kettering became interested in the possibility that Bob had discovered a diagnostic test for cancer. It turned out however that anyone who was sick tested positive. Much of the work Bob did at Sloan Kettering he called biochemical genetics. He became convinced that the proper treatment for leukemia was to use two therapeutic agents simultaneously, a protocol considered too radical at that time. Years later it became standard practice. Bob proceeded to develop a specific screening program to look for drugs that could be used in combination. Although he did not succeed in developing a cure for leukemia, his experience at Sloan Kettering laid the groundwork for his development of the test for PKU.

In 1954 Bob was offered a more lucrative position at Roswell Park in Buffalo, New York. The Guthries began house hunting in that area, ultimately moving to Williamsville, a suburb with a small-town quality. The town was originally founded in the early 1880s in the vicinity of a water-wheel-powered flour mill and was known for its excellent schools. Bob no longer had the commuting problem he had come to dread in Staten Island. In 1956 Jim was born, bringing the total to five young Guthries for Margaret to tend.

At Roswell Park Bob had a laboratory of his own and lab assistants to help with the work. He began doing research with freshwater sponges. He also continued to do research on cancer, working to identify drugs for the treatment of childhood leukemia. More convinced than ever that combination therapy was the way to go, he developed a screening method to look for compounds that could be used in combination with two compounds that were already known to work initially in acute childhood leukemia—methotrexate or a-methopterin and 6-mercaptopurine. He tested hundreds of compounds to find one that would show what is called "collateral sensitivity." Hopes were raised when he found a compound that was effective in treating mice that had leukemia. However it had no effect on the disease in human subjects. It only made the patients sleepy. Bob continued to be unsuccessful in convincing clinicians he knew to try combination therapy. After he left Roswell Park, combination therapy became accepted practice and approximately half of their childhood leukemia patients were cured.

One of Bob's colleagues at the new lab was Dr. Howard Tieckelmann, later to become head of the department of chemistry at the University of Buffalo. The two men worked together to find chemotherapeutic agents to fight cancer and did research to isolate unknown compounds in urine and blood that might be related to the causes of mental retardation and developmental disabilities in children. Howard was a kindred spirit, another night person. In the evening on his way home from Roswell Park, Bob would stop at the chemistry building (locked after ten p.m.), go in through a basement window and find Howard working with his graduate students.

The Guthries' second son John was a cause of continuing concern for them. He had never developed normally and they had finally accepted the fact that he was mentally retarded. In Buffalo they became acquainted with the Sunshine League, an organization of parents of mentally retarded children. Eventually Bob was given a small grant by the Sunshine League allowing him to hire a full-time technician by the name of Ada Susi. He also hired a part-time assistant, Mrs. Sally Bloom. These two loyal women worked many years for Bob and contributed a great deal to his success.

Although Sally did not have a child with disabilities, she was the vice-president of the Erie County Chapter of the New York Association for Retarded Children (now called the Association for Retarded Citizens). Since she did not have a background in science Sally was given the job of collecting urine specimens from families in which the parents were unaffected while two or more children were mentally retarded. Bob used the urine specimens in his research, looking for new causes of mental retardation.

After several years at Roswell Park, Bob met Dr. Mitchell Rubin, head of pediatrics at Children's Hospital in Buffalo and the University of Buffalo Medical School. Dr. Rubin was interested in Bob's idea of using microorganisms in the laboratory to study human biochemical genetics related to mental retardation. Eventually Dr. Rubin asked Bob if he knew anyone with similar interests who might want to join the pediatric staff. Bob contacted a former protege from the Sloan Kettering Institute who came to Buffalo to look over the pediatrics department. Bob escorted him around the hospital and in the process became better acquainted with the staff himself. The position did not materialize for his friend; however later there was an opening on the pediatric staff. Bob took the position and moved from Roswell Park to Buffalo Children's Hospital in 1958. Here Bob found his niche and here he remained for the rest of his professional career.

Once more the Guthrie family grew. Patty completed the family in 1958 and the family moved to a larger house in Williamsville where they remained until 1995.

Asbjörn Fölling, 1888–1973, discoverer of
phenylketonuria in 1934.

2

PKU—What's That?*

The year was 1934. The harried young mother entered the doctor's office with her two blond-haired, blue-eyed children who were mentally retarded. According to Drs. Siegried and Willard Centerwall's account, the little girl was seven years old and had not walked until she was almost two. She had a vocabulary of only a few words. Her brother, three years younger, had also developed slowly and had never learned to walk or talk. The mother had gone from one doctor to another in hopes of finding someone who could help her children. When none of the eminent child specialists could identify the problem, she had desperately turned to questionable healers, all to no avail.

Dr. Asbjörn Fölling had been suggested by one of her husband's colleagues. A physician and biochemist at the University of Oslo School of Medicine in Norway, he had written his medical thesis on "Mechanisms of Acidosis," but he did not usually treat patients. The mother insisted however. She recited the litany of their symptoms. One especially disconcerting symptom was that her children

*The following history of PKU is based in part on an article in the Spring/Summer 1992 issue of the *National PKU News*, on the book *Phenylketonuria* edited by Frank L. Lyman, M.D., published by Charles C. Thomas and on an abstract by John W. Gerard.

19

had a strange musty odor. Their hair and skin, and especially their urine, smelled. Worse yet, the odor that clung to them aggravated her husband's asthma. She did not mention it to Dr. Fölling, but one of the doctors she had consulted had sent her to a psychiatrist because of her "illusions" about the smell of her children's urine.

With his interest in science and his concern for this desperate family Dr. Fölling decided to study their problem. Theorizing that the children might have a chronic infection, he examined samples of their urine, finding that it did indeed have a strong musty odor, but there was no evidence of infection. He thus decided to test for diacetic acid by adding ten percent ferric chloride to the urine, expecting the mixture to turn a red-brown color. To his surprise it turned green. Knowing that adrenaline gives a similar green color with ferric chloride, he tested for adrenaline but found none.

Intrigued by the challenge Dr. Fölling asked the mother for more urine. She returned with 20 liters and Dr. Fölling began working relentlessly to isolate the chemical that caused the strange reaction. He thought it just might be related to the children's mental disabilities. Dr. Fölling worked for seven weeks and after many complications he extracted a pure product which he found to be phenylpyruvic acid.

He still did not have an answer for the mother, but he used the same test on the urine of several hundred patients in institutions for the mentally retarded, finding eight other similar cases. Interestingly, four of the patients were siblings, suggesting that the disorder might be genetic in origin. Based on these findings he published a landmark paper in 1934, five months after his first visit with the mother and her children. Dr. Fölling called the disorder he had described "imbecillitas phenylpyruvica" because it caused mental retardation and phenylpyruvic acid was present in the urine. Scientists later changed the name of the disorder to phenylketonuria or PKU.

Dr. Fölling could have rested on his laurels after his discovery, but he continued to do research on the newly discovered disease and in the process managed to challenge the imaginations of the many scientists who are now leading the attack on this and other metabolic disorders. In 1962 Dr. Folling was given the first International Kennedy Award for his work, with the presentation made in person by President John Kennedy. Present at the ceremony was the author Pearl Buck who had written *The Child Who Never Grew* about her only daughter who had PKU. Also attending were movie personalities Burt Lancaster and Judy Garland, who had co-starred in a short movie about mental retardation. The film *A Child is Waiting* was shown at the ceremony and Bob Guthrie reported that when the film ended and the lights came on Burt Lancaster was wiping away a tear.

Dr. Folling's discovery spurred research on PKU. Dr. George Jervis of New York soon reported that patients with PKU have a hereditary enzymatic defect in which the liver is unable to properly break down phenylalanine (an essential amino acid present in all protein-containing food) into tyrosine and other substances that the body can use. Later researchers demonstrated that these patients lack the enzyme phenylalanine hydroxylase which in normal individuals converts phenylalanine to tyrosine. Dr. Jervis found that the result is the build-up of phenylalanine in the body of those with PKU and the excretion of phenylpyruvic acid in their sweat and urine. This transforms into phenylacetic acid causing the typical musty odor. However, the odor and the typical eczema are the least of the worries for the families of PKU patients. With the build-up of phenylalanine the baby gradually becomes less responsive. Its development becomes more and more delayed until usually by about two years of age it is found to be mentally retarded.

Professor Horst Bickel of Germany is another pioneer in the field of PKU. As with Dr. Fölling, it took a persistent determined mother to spur him to action. In 1951 Dr. Bickel was a research fellow on the staff at the Children's Hospital in Birmingham, England. A 17-month-old girl with mental retardation was brought to the clinic and Professor Bickel, especially interested in studying PKU, found her urine tested positive with ferric chloride. Having made the diagnosis Dr. Bickel wanted to study her, but at that time there was no treatment for the disorder. The child's mother was unconsoled and could not understand why he could not help her daughter when he had made the diagnosis. Thereafter each morning when he reported for work Dr. Bickel was confronted at the hospital entrance by the child's mother. The child was severely handicapped, unable to stand, walk or talk. She showed no interest in her food or surroundings, spending most of her time moaning, crying and banging her head. Dr. Bickel tried to explain that nothing could be done, but the mother persisted. The situation became so stressful that the professor started using different entrances to the hospital in an effort to avoid the daily confrontation.

Finally realizing he could not elude this tenacious woman, Dr. Bickel tried to reduce the child's phenylalanine by using glutamic acid. The attempted treatment was unsuccessful. Finally he and his colleagues, Evelyn Hickmans and John Gerrard, consulted their friend Dr. Louis Woolf at the Great Ormond Street Hospital in London. They speculated that the child's mental retardation might have something to do with the high levels of phenylalanine in her system and discussed the possibility of treating her with a low phenylalanine diet.

Dr. Woolf had had a theory for some time that it might be possible to treat PKU with diet. As a researcher with a Ph.D., he was unable to treat patients and test his theory. A recent report had been published that showed that it was possible to remove the amino acids—phenylalanine, tryptophane, tyrosine and cysteine—from a protein hydrolysate (produced from any protein) by filtering it through activated charcoal. Dr. Woolf had access to casein hydrolysate because he had worked for a company that was producing it in the event that when World War II ended there would be a demand for such a product for people suffering from severe malnutrition.

Years later Horst Bickel admitted to Dr. Woolf that at the time he thought Louis was a little crazy in thinking dietary treatment feasible. Nevertheless Horst Bickel and Evelyn Hickmans wasted no time in beginning their work in the laboratory. After the amino acids had been filtered out of a casein hydrolysate, all of them—except the phenylalanine—were returned and a phenylalanine-free formula had been produced. The process was time-consuming and difficult. It had to be done in a cold room or the mixture would spoil. The charcoal got on everything. Professor Bickel's figure wrapped in layers of sweaters, topped by a charcoal-smudged lab coat, became a common sight at the hospital. He distinctly remembered one cold Christmas Eve having to remain at work in his frigid lab while his family enjoyed a warm Christmas celebration at home without him.

After the formula was developed, the child of the persistent mother was admitted to the hospital. Although Professor Bickel encountered opposition to his plans to institute this untested treatment, she was started on the new product. It was soon found that she did not do well on the phenylalanine-free formula. Since phenylalanine is an essential amino acid she needed enough of it in her formula for her to grow and develop, but not so much that she became hyperphenylalaninemic. Thereafter phenylalanine was added to her diet in the form of small amounts of precisely measured whole milk. The child was then discharged from the hospital and Professor Bickel began to make a weekly supply of the product which the mother picked up at the hospital. Gradually the child began to improve. Her eyes became brighter, her hair grew darker, she no longer cried continuously and she stopped banging her head. She even learned to crawl, to stand and to climb on chairs.

In order to determine whether the improvement noted by the mother was real and whether such progress could be attributed to the special diet, Professor Bickel began to add five grams of phenylalanine to the daily supply of the product without the knowledge of the mother. Within two days the mother reported tearfully that something was wrong with the new supply of formula. Her child had lost nearly all of the ground she had gained. Within six hours of starting the fresh supply her daughter had begun to cry and to bang her head and within 24 hours she could no longer stand and could scarcely crawl.

Professor Bickel admitted to her what he and his colleagues had done. He explained that in view of the expense of producing the product it was very important to determine its efficacy in a hospital setting where there could be close clinical observation and biochemical findings could be recorded. The mother agreed and the child was again admitted to the hospital. After a period of observation on the low-phenylalanine diet, four grams of phenylalanine were added to her diet daily. Within 24 hours she became irritable and drowsy. She lost interest in her food and surroundings, developed facial eczema and salivated profusely. She vomited repeatedly and by the sixth day she could no longer stand or crawl. The additional phenylalanine was then discontinued and within three weeks she had almost completely recovered. Although the child still had mental retardation, her improvement was undeniable.

Professor Bickel and his colleagues had trouble publishing their findings. The conclusions were considered "too speculative" and one well-known child specialist scoffed at the suggestion that modifying the diet could have any influence on a child's behavior. But the journal *Lancet* agreed to publish a preliminary communication. Later a full article was published in *Acta Paediatrica* in 1953. This spurred increased interest by the medical community in PKU.

The next breakthrough in PKU came in 1957 when Dr. Willard Centerwall of Los Angeles, himself the father of a child with mental retardation, developed the first diagnostic screening test for the disorder. It was standard practice in testing urine for the presence of phenylpyruvic acid to enhance the chemical reaction by adding hydrochloric acid to the sample before adding the ferric chloride. Dr. Centerwall discovered that the phenypyruvic acid could be detected without first acidifying the urine. A solution of ferric chloride would produce a green color when applied to a wet diaper if there was an excessive amount of phenypyruvic acid in the urine. This was a significant discovery. It eliminated the necessity of collecting a urine sample and sending it to a laboratory to make the diagnosis. This diaper test was the first step toward mass screening for PKU. Dr.

Centerwall's discovery made it possible for doctors to do the test routinely in their offices. The diaper test was done when the child was five or six weeks of age to allow enough time for the phenylalanine to build up in the baby's system and to spill over into the urine as phenylpyruvic acid should the child have PKU.

Dr. Centerwall's diaper test and Dr. Bickel's research sparked a flurry of activity in diagnosis, treatment and genetic counseling. Projects were initiated in which all of the residents of institutions for the mentally retarded were tested. It was found that one percent of these individuals had PKU. It was through such testing that Pearl Buck's daughter was found to have PKU. Doctors began testing all of their patients who had mental retardation and were encouraged to include the diaper test in their routine care for all infants.

There were differences of opinion among doctors about testing. Some tested only fair-skinned, blond-haired babies since light skin and blonde hair are some of the symptoms of PKU. Others tested only those who had an older sibling who had PKU. One faculty member of a well-known medical school declared that the diet was a placebo and that the seeming improvement was just due to the extra attention given to the babies. He stated that PKU patients should be given tyrosine supplements but no special diet. He received a lot of publicity at first, but his hypothesis was disproved when the one PKU patient he treated with a tyrosine supplement developed mental retardation. Most responsible doctors who read the literature began testing every baby for PKU.

It was found that the incidence of PKU in the general population is one in 15,000, but that the incidence varies in different ethnic groups. Among the Irish and Scottish the occurrence is as high as one in 5,000, while among Blacks, Finns and Ashkenazi Jews it is quite rare, perhaps as low as one in 300,000. PKU was found to be inherited as a Mendelian recessive condition, meaning that both parents carry a recessive gene for PKU. These carriers are completely normal, but among their offspring the probability is that one in four will have PKU, two in four will also be carriers of the defective gene and one child of the four will be normal. These figures are mathematical probabilities, however, and do not always occur. In some families the only two children will have PKU. In others only one of five has it. And of course in some families where both parents are carriers of the defect, none of the children will have PKU and the parents will not even know that they are carriers.

The next significant development in the PKU story occurred in 1961 when Robert Guthrie, also the parent of a child with mental retardation, developed a simple blood test in which an elevated blood phenylalanine level could be detected soon after birth. The Guthrie test turned out to be significantly more accurate than the diaper test and it had the advantage of diagnosing the disorder early enough so that an infant could be put on the special diet before any brain damage had occurred.

From 1964 to 1982, 170 children with PKU participated in the "Collaborative Study of Children with PKU" headed by Dr. Richard Koch of Los Angeles. This study concluded that if the diet is started within 14 days after birth and is carefully adhered to, and if the phenylalanine level is normalized and monitored, the children with PKU have essentially the same development as other children. It was also discovered that if there is a delay beyond two weeks of age in diagnosis and treatment, there is some loss of later IQ. By the end of the 1960s clinicians working in the PKU field estimated that babies who have PKU lose one IQ point for each week they are untreated during their first year of life.

By this time a number of different food products had been developed for children with PKU. Nutritionists had become important members of the team of professionals that dealt with the parents of these children. As Professor Bickel reported, since phenylalanine is an essential amino acid, a person with PKU must have some of it in order to grow and develop properly. The amount must be precisely balanced to provide enough, but not too much, to the system.

Increasingly parents and professionals are working with each other to make life easier for persons with PKU. One such example is nutritionist Virginia Schuett. Originally she had a grant for a year from the federal government to set up a national registry of all PKU clinics, but she is better known for the cookbook she produced that is widely used by families dealing with PKU. It had been her dream also to start a PKU newsletter. She had a difficult time getting funding for this project and finally grubstaked it with funds from the revised edition of her cookbook. The first edition of the newsletter went out in 1989 to many organizations and individuals and was very well received. It provided lots of good information and was a way of uniting families who were geographically isolated from others who were dealing with the disorder. The newsletter was a success and has been published twice a year since then. It has a number of associate editors, one of whom was Bob Guthrie who wrote about what was going on nationally and internationally in the PKU field.

With the advent of PKU screening and the availability of the medical food product in all developed countries doctors, nurses and nutritionists could help PKU patients develop normally. The medical community congratulated itself on having solved another mystery regarding one of the causes of mental retardation and on having the tools to prevent its disastrous effects. However they were surprised and chagrined when girls with PKU began reaching child-bearing age. Since in the past girls with PKU had become severely retarded with most of them ending up in institutions, they did not have children. After the diaper test was developed and the newborn screening began, girls who were diagnosed and treated became part of the so-called normal population.

At first, testing was not routine and was done only in institutions for the retarded, in child development clinics and in cases where PKU was suspected, usually because an older sibling had already been diagnosed with the disorder. Thus some of the girls who were first diagnosed with PKU had already suffered some of the effects of the disorder at the time of their diagnosis and had developed mild retardation. In addition, when doctors began treating PKU it was thought patients could safely discontinue the diet during early childhood. No one knew for sure when the stringent diet could safely be discontinued, but many professionals felt that after the child's brain had fully developed, probably sometime between the age of six to eight years, it was no longer necessary. Thus many of the women who had been diagnosed with PKU in the early years were off the diet long before reaching adulthood. Some of them had memories of being on a special diet for a while, but some did not even know they had PKU.

Subsequently, obstetricians began seeing women with PKU who were not on diet. To their dismay they found that 95 percent of the babies born to these women had serious abnormalities including heart malformation, microcephaly and mental retardation. It appeared that all the progress achieved by the screening test and the treatment would be nullified by the numbers of children with mental retardation born to women with PKU. Some physicians had always suspected that persons with PKU, especially girls, should be kept on the diet at least through their child-bearing years, probably for their entire lifetime.

A maternal PKU study was begun in 1984, financed by the National Institute of Child Health and Human Development to determine whether women with PKU who were on the diet during pregnancy would produce normal offspring and, if this was possible, when the diet should be started and how strict it should be. The study, which includes the United States, Canada and Germany is just being completed. So far, it has been determined that if a woman with PKU adheres to the phenylalanine-restricted diet, takes her phenylalanine-restricted protein product and keeps her phenylalanine level between 2 to 6 mg. percent, her offspring will have a normal potential. It is recommended that the diet be instituted prior to conception if the woman has not been on a phenylalanine-restricted diet with good control.

Maternal PKU camps are a wave of the future for girls with PKU. These camps, started in California in 1990, follow the same concept that diabetic camps do for children with diabetes. The first ones were held during the summer at the campus of the University of California at Davis for girls 13 years old and older. They stay together in a college dormitory, enjoy social and sports activities and get to meet others who have PKU. There are counselors with whom they can discuss their problems. Nutritionists teach them how to prepare new food products they can use. They are served tasty well-balanced, low-phenylalanine foods and shown how to keep charts of the foods they eat so that they can take more responsibility in adhering to their diets.

Most important of all, they learn more about PKU and why it is vital for them to stay on diet, especially when they are planning a pregnancy. One young woman, Dianne Obert, who was one of the first infants diagnosed and successfully treated in the Los Angeles area, attended the first maternal PKU camp. She was off diet at the time but was so impressed that she went back on diet and became a staunch supporter of the camps. She has since become a camp counselor and writes about the camps in the PKU newsletter. The camps are expensive and take a lot of planning, but the idea has spread to Massachusetts and similar camps are in the works for other states.

Dealing with teenagers who have PKU is often difficult for parents and professionals alike. Adolescents are testing limits and what better way to test than to enjoy a hamburger with their friends. It is difficult for them to see that straying from the diet has any effect on them. Most of them feel well and the long-term effects of diet discontinuation do not become evident until many years later. Some of the girls are especially proud of their blond hair and are appalled to find their hair darkening when they go on diet. One shock treatment is for them to see a person with untreated PKU who is severely handicapped. This often makes believers of them.

Research on PKU continues, but it was Dr. Guthrie's development of the screening test that paved the way for a whole battery of tests that can detect treatable disorders in newborn infants. This was the beginning of newborn screening for the prevention of disease in children.

front

PLEASE PRINT

388976

FEP PROGRAM DEPT OF PEDIATRICS
SUNY
BUFFALO, NEW YORK 14214 NO. F104976

DATE:_____

☐ NORMAL   ☐ ABNORMAL

PATIENT'S NAME _____

ADDRESS _____

BIRTH DATE _____

COUNTY _____

DOCTOR'S NAME _____

ADDRESS _____

TELEPHONE _____

SATURATE CIRCLES

◯ ◯ ◯

---

back

INSTRUCTIONS

1. PLEASE PRINT WITH BALL POINT PEN AND FILL IN ALL SECTIONS OF FILTER PAPER.

2. After skin is sterilized, puncture with sterile Lancet.

3. Bleeding is assisted by making limb dependent.

4. Completely fill each circle with a single application of blood. **Do not apply blood a second time to same spot.**

5. Allow spots to dry completely.

6. S & S® No. 903™ Lot # W-32

◯ ◯ ◯

Filter paper cards for PKU testing

3

A Newborn Screening Test

In 1957 Robert Guthrie served as vice president of the Erie County Chapter of the National Association for Retarded Children (NARC). Because of his son Johnny, Bob had become deeply interested in doing research that might lead to the prevention of mental retardation caused by errors of metabolism. So for one of the chapter meetings he invited a speaker from the University of Buffalo Children's Hospital, Dr. Robert Warner, director of the Children's Rehabilitation Center, a diagnostic and evaluation center for mental retardation. Dr. Mitchell Rubin, chair of the department of pediatrics at the same hospital, introduced Dr. Warner, who talked about his patients who had developmental disabilities.

After the meeting Bob discussed his ideas with Dr. Warner and Dr. Rubin. As a result Bob kept in touch with Dr. Warner, and the following year Dr. Warner introduced him to PKU, explaining that this was an inborn error of phenylalanine metabolism that caused mental retardation. He explained what Professor Horst Bickel in Germany several years earlier had found that when these children were on a special phenylalanine-restricted diet, their blood phenylalanine levels were lower and their behavior greatly improved.

One of Dr. Warner's problems in administering the diet was the difficulty in closely monitoring blood phenylalanine levels in his patients, essential if he was to alter their diets when necessary. The tests for the monitoring were laborious. He was having to send 15 to 20 cc of venous blood to a firm in California each time he tested a patient. He proposed that Bob devise a simpler method for measuring blood phenylalanine. So began Bob's phenomenal research in developing tests for inborn errors of metabolism.

Bob told Drs. Warner and Rubin that he would work with bugs to find a cure for mental retardation. In three days he reported to Dr. Warner he could now do the test using three to five drops of capillary blood from a finger prick. This was much easier than obtaining a venous blood sample, an especially difficult procedure with young children. What he had done seemed simple to Bob. He had already been using a method for measuring substances in blood samples from cancer patients by putting filter paper discs on agar surfaces and screening for certain compounds. His technique utilized bacterial metabolism. For testing phenylalanine he used a spot of blood serum on a filter paper disc that he put on the surface of an agar culture gel which contained a specific substance to inhibit the growth of bacteria but which was reversed by phenylalanine. If excess phenylalanine was present in the blood, it removed the growth inhibition and bacteria would grow.

After overnight incubation he could examine the sample and compare the diameter of the growth zone around it with that of a "control" disc of blood serum to which he had added known quantities of phenylalanine. The agar remained clear except for the circles of growth surrounding discs that contained phenylalanine. In this way he could tell how much phenylalanine was in a sample by comparing it to his control sample. Thus Bob had developed a simple method of monitoring blood phenylalanine that involved only a few drops of blood. The principle was identical to that of the bacterial assays he had used for cancer patients. He called the technique "bacterial inhibition assay" or BIA.

For the next four years Dr. Warner used this test, continuing his pioneering efforts to treat more and more children with PKU. Unfortunately, all the children he treated were already mentally disabled because the diagnosis had not been made in time to prevent the symptoms of the disorder. The urine test then in use for diagnosis of PKU was not reliable until the infant was several weeks old and the phenylalanine had built up in the infant's system, spilling over into its urine. Most of the time clinicians did not even test an infant for PKU unless it started to show signs of developmental delay or an older child in the same family had previously been diagnosed with PKU.

In 1958 Bob was asked by Dr. Rubin to join the pediatrics department at the Children's Hospital. He left Roswell Park Memorial Institute and continued to pursue his interests in biochemical research, primarily looking for new inherited metabolic diseases similar to PKU that might be associated with mental retardation in children. He was not really interested in PKU per se, except as a model.

Bob began to use many different microbial inhibitors from among the hundreds that had been synthesized for use in cancer chemotherapy. Each of these could be used for an inhibition assay similar in principle to the one he was already using for measuring phenylalanine in PKU. For his research Bob used urine from children who were mentally retarded and who had a sibling also known to be mentally handicapped but who had parents who were not disabled. He did a reverse inhibition assay, putting the urine in the agar and putting filter paper discs of different inhibitors on the agar. If the inhibition around a disc was abolished and bacteria grew, he knew that something in the urine was probably an antagonist of the inhibitor in that disc. Bob's lab must have looked strange to anyone expecting to find a room full of scientific equipment. His agar trays were regular Pyrex baking dishes such as any homemaker had in her kitchen.

Bob continued this research approach from 1958 to 1961 when an amazing coincidence occurred. He learned that Margaret Doll, a baby born to his wife's sister a thousand miles away in Minneapolis, had been diagnosed at 15 months of age as having PKU. She was developmentally delayed, leading a pediatric psychiatrist to check her urine with the ferric chloride test for PKU then in use. The test

33

was positive. Bob went to Minneapolis and tested the child's blood with his inhibition assay, finding that she was indeed positive.

Also in 1961 Bob went with his mother to a small town in Alberta, Canada, for a family funeral. While he was there he became acquainted with a doctor who asked him what he did professionally. When Bob mentioned PKU, the doctor indicated that he had his nurse routinely test every infant he saw in his office with the urine ferric chloride test. The supplies for the test were sent to every doctor in the province by the College of Physicians.

These two experiences led Bob to renew his interest in the possibility of screening all infants for PKU with a blood phenylalanine test. It was clear that the sooner dietary treatment began, the better the prognosis for intellectual growth. He had always done the test using liquid blood serum collected in capillary tubes and then transferred to filter paper discs. At this point it occurred to him that it might simplify the test if whole blood was collected by simply blotting a piece of filter paper directly on a small heel puncture wound. He tried the procedure using a paper punch from the office to make a small disc from a dried-blood sample and proceeding as usual with the rest of the test. The filter paper test was compared with the capillary blood test and found to be accurate! He was able to do the test using a quarter-inch disc of blood-impregnated filter paper. As far as Bob was able to determine no one in the history of medicine had ever used dried spots of blood on filter paper to obtain a quantitative sample for testing for any purpose. The test turned out to be more successful than he would ever have dared to dream!

Bob was convinced that the easiest way to make sure that every infant was screened for PKU was to get blood samples from babies before they left the hospital. The technique he recommended was to prick the infant's heel and then blot the drops of blood with a filter paper that could be dried and sent to his laboratory. He was not sure however if the blood phenylalanine rose quickly enough in a newborn infant to detect PKU by the time the baby was discharged from the hospital. From publications and from private correspondence he was able to obtain information on only six infants with PKU concerning their blood phenylalanine levels in the first few days of life. The data were encouraging and seemed to indicate that phenylalanine did rise quickly enough to be detected at this early stage. Bob's next step was a pilot project to test his procedure.

The obvious place to test a high-risk population was at an institution for people with mental disabilities. At the Newark State School near Rochester, New York, Bob was told that all their admissions were tested and that the medical staff was familiar with all of their PKU cases. Bob's research and his active participation in NARC had gained him many contacts—which he used. A friend by the name of Mrs. Bergeron had a son who had been diagnosed with PKU at 13 months of age by Dr. Warner. The child had shown an unexpected beneficial response to the diet, although his development at the time of his diagnosis had been unmeasurable.

Mrs. Bergeron was motivated to form a group for parents of children with PKU. As a result of a newspaper article about the group, the mother of four children with mental disabilities called Mrs. Bergeron, who in turn put her in touch with Dr. Warner. The physician found that all four of her children had PKU. One of the children had been placed in the Newark State School when she turned eleven. Oddly enough, the staff at Newark State School did not know that this little girl had PKU. When this was discovered they quickly decided to coöperate with Bob in screening all the residents of the institution to see if they had any other undiagnosed cases.

During the summer of 1961 two university students worked at the Newark State School collecting the dried spots of blood from some 3,000 residents and mailing them to Bob's laboratory. At the same time they performed urine tests with ferric chloride but did not reveal their results to Bob as a check on the efficiency of his test. As a result Bob and his assistants, Ada and Karl Susi, found 23 cases of PKU at Newark—four more than had been discovered by urine testing.

That fall Bob gave a talk about PKU to the Association for Retarded Children at Jamestown, New York. By then he was convinced that his test was going to be used to screen all infants so he devoted most of his talk to that subject. A few days after the talk he began to receive filter paper specimens of blood from newborn infants in two Jamestown hospitals. Thus newborn screening had its start in 1961 in Jamestown, New York.

Another coincidence occurred. Each year the National Association for Retarded Children selects a poster child for their publicity. In 1961 they had two poster children—siblings with PKU. Sheila had mental handicaps while her younger sister Kammy who had been diagnosed at birth and placed on the diet immediately was developing normally. Of course Kammy was diagnosed because of her older sister's mental retardation. The poster bore an inscription saying there was hope for the mentally retarded.

Since Bob had received a small grant from the NARC for his research, Dr. Elizabeth Boggs, president of NARC pressed him to publish his screening test in a medical journal as soon as possible. His test could then be legitimately used for publicity with the message that an NARC grantee had produced a test for screening newborn infants for PKU. Bob prepared a short paper and with Dr. Rubin's help it was published as a "Letter to the Editor" in the *Journal of the American Medical Association* in October 1961. That same month the NARC held a press conference at its annual meeting in San Francisco to publicize Bob's test. There he posed for pictures with Kammy to begin the NARC publicity campaign supporting universal testing of newborn babies for PKU. And so Bob began his career as a traveling salesman for PKU screening.

Excitement grew at Children's Hospital in Buffalo. *Life* magazine became interested and sent a reporter and photographer to interview and photograph Bob at his laboratory. The following January an article about the new screening test to detect PKU in newborn infants appeared in *Life* along with pictures of Bob and of the two sisters, Sheila and Kammy. Up to that time Bob had not had the opportunity to do many tests, but this national publicity undoubtedly influenced the federal government to fund a trial of the test.

Bob and his assistants had set up an exhibit of the test at the October 1961 annual meeting of the American Public Health Association (APHA) in Detroit. There Dr. Arthur Lesser, director of the maternal and child health service of the U.S. Children's Bureau, met them with many questions about the test such as, "How many infants should be tested for a trial?" If the results indicated that PKU occurred as frequently as one in 10,000 births, as Bob thought, instead of one in 20,000 or 40,000 as recorded in the literature, then screening 400,000 infants would reveal 40 cases. It was decided that number would be sufficient for a trial.

Ultimately Dr. Lesser agreed to support Bob's proposal and arranged to award a grant allowing him to prepare all the materials and organize and administer a trial of the test for 400,000 infants. The Children's Bureau offered to pay the cost of sending personnel from every state health department in the country to Buffalo to be trained in the use of the test. At that time the Children's Bureau was amply funded, particularly for projects to prevent mental retardation because of the influence of President John F. Kennedy, who had a sister with mental retardation. Twenty-nine states agreed to participate. Meanwhile, early in 1962 the Erie County Department of Health and the neighboring Niagara County Health Department set up the PKU test and began to offer it to the hospitals in their areas. That spring the first infant with PKU was detected in Niagara County after 800 infants had been screened.

With the funds from the Children's Bureau, Bob rented a house near Children's Hospital which became known as the PKU Cottage. This was transformed into a miniature factory where some 24 people prepared enough test kits for all laboratories to have uniform materials. The kits were packed in a small cardboard box and a printer prepared one million filter papers with serial numbers for distribution to the health departments.

Since this preparation required collating and packaging, Bob suggested that the printer arrange for this work to be done at a sheltered workshop for adults with mental disabilities in Buffalo. Some

20 of these people were employed on this project for about three months. A label from NARC was put on each package with the message: "Retarded children can be helped." Each kit also included a NARC brochure with the picture of the two poster children with PKU and a message about the test. The goal was to package the test so that everything would be instant, like instant coffee. In that way the laboratories testing for PKU would not have to employ trained bacteriologists. They could easily mix the ingredients and perform the test with existing personnel.

Initially each PKU test kit box contained enough material for 100 tests. Later the amount of material was increased to allow for 500 tests. In each cardboard box were the following ingredients of the bacterial inhibition assay: (1) a seven-by-eleven-inch plastic tray (these were trays were originally manufactured to display jewelry and were used for the same purpose the Pyrex baking dishes served in Bob's lab); (2) a bottle of simple glucose-salt powder to be used as a culture medium; (3) a bottle of agar powder to be combined with the culture medium powder; (4) a small vial containing the exact amount of B-2-thienylalanine inhibitor; (5) another small vial containing powdered spores of *Bacillus subtilis;* (6) a strip of filter paper containing spots of dried blood, each with a known different quantity of phenylalanine (2, 4, 6, 8, 10, 12 and 20 mg/dl) to be used as standards; and (7) instructions for performing and interpreting the test. A normal phenylalanine level was considered to be a little less than 2 mg/dl.

For 17 years Bob had not done any sailing, but when he rented the PKU Cottage he found an old sailboat sitting outside. Every day he stepped around it to get to the house. When his curiosity got the better of him, he inquired and discovered that it belonged to a woman whose husband had crewed on a racing sailboat but no longer used it. Bob asked if she would rent it to him for the summer for $100. She replied that for $100 he could have it. He bought a trailer for the boat and an old sail that blew out. There wasn't much time for sailing that summer anyway.

The first few weeks of 1962 were busy ones for Bob and his chief technician, Mrs. Susi. During that period they trained approximately 60 technicians from 29 states in the use of the test. Each course lasted five days. Following the training each technician was supplied with boxes of test ingredients. They also received filter papers for collecting the blood specimens so that all of the tests would be the same. Finally they were supplied with filter papers for collecting urine when the infants were four weeks old so that urine test results on these infants could be compared with the results of the blood tests.

Dr. Robert A. MacCready, the state laboratory director for Massachusetts, was so interested that he came to Buffalo to take Bob's training course personally—instead of sending a technician. Dr. MacCready became an ardent supporter of newborn screening and was determined to test all babies born in Massachusetts, not just the 10,000 that were allocated to him as his share of the 400,000. He had the good fortune of discovering a case after the first 1,000 tests, three cases after the first 8,000 and nine cases after 54,000 tests. Each time a case was found, he publicized it throughout the state to arouse interest. As a result, within six months after testing began, every hospital in Massachusetts was sending in specimens.

Overall, Bob and his assistants distributed enough material to test a million infants. Within two years 400,000 infants were tested in the 29 states that participated and 39 cases of PKU were found— an incidence of about one per 10,000, confirming Bob's estimate. Not one case was missed by the screening. The conclusion was that the newborn screening test had had a truly successful trial. Of the 400,000 infants screened in the national program, 165,000—more than one third—were in Massachusetts. This could only be attributed to Dr. MacCready's enthusiasm. Furthermore, of the 39 infants with PKU identified in the national program, ten were from Massachusetts. By 1963 the Massachusetts legislature had passed a law requiring the test on all infants. Oregon became the second state to institute newborn screening and later other state legislatures passed laws requiring newborn screening for PKU.

The test was not without its detractors. Some researchers claimed it was not accurate. An article appeared in *The Atlantic Monthly* declaring that Bob Guthrie and Bob Warner should be in jail for wrongly diagnosing many people with PKU. In fact, Massachusetts was the only state in which the proposal was not opposed by the state medical society. Some professionals were not as enthusiastic about the Guthrie test as was Dr. MacCready. Bob encountered a great deal of difficulty in getting an article about the test accepted for publication in a medical journal. This resistance presented itself as a challenge to Bob who accepted every opportunity to speak at meetings about the need for screening. He traveled the length and breadth of the United States as well as overseas always emphasizing the simplicity of the test.

In 1962 Bob had an interesting experience in Lisbon, Portugal where he had an exhibit of his test at the International Pediatrics Convention. A husband and wife, both medical doctors, had a child with mental retardation. They stopped at his exhibit and asked if he could test their child for PKU. He gave them a piece of filter paper and on the last night of the meeting they returned with the blood sample. Bob took it with him to Marseilles, France, where he was to spend a few days in the home of a friend. He set up his equipment in the friend's kitchen and did the test. The child did not have PKU, but Bob had demonstrated to himself the simplicity of the test.

Lay groups and professional organizations invited him to speak. To his surprise Bob received the most positive responses from non-physicians. After seemingly endless delays, in 1963 the professional journal *Pediatrics* finally agreed to publish Bob's method. The NARC played an important role in spreading the word about the PKU test and the need for screening. Dr. MacCready was then the public health and prevention committee chair for the organization. After following the course of the test for a year or two, the committee recommended to NARC that they advise the state chapters to press for mandatory state laws such as the one passed in Massachusetts. This campaign led to further opposition, often from the medical profession.

In states where the medical society expressed an opinion, it was invariably in opposition to a law. The reasoning was that the state should not be dictating how a doctor should practice medicine. When a bill mandating PKU screening was proposed in the California legislature, the state medical association sent a representative to Sacramento to testify in opposition. Nevertheless the momentum carried the message forward and by 1966 PKU screening was mandatory in the majority of the states. This would not have happened without the hard work of the parents of children with disabilities and the determination of Dr. Robert Guthrie.

Back in his laboratory Bob was busy developing tests for other disorders that could be treated to prevent mental retardation. Eventually he and his laboratory personnel developed tests for over 30 different treatable conditions that cause mental retardation or death. All 30 could be applied to the single newborn blood specimen originally collected only for PKU screening. Not all of these tests have been practical, as some of the disorders are very rare, but at least six have been crucial.

Bob Guthrie in his lab

4

In the Lawyers' Den

After all of Bob Guthrie's hard work and his monumental accomplishment, one would like to think that he was given due credit and honor and everyone lived happily ever after. That was not to be. In Bob's case invention was the mother of necessity. The test he had developed was a triumph over a devastating disorder, but he needed someone to guide him through the intricacies of patent applications and marketing agreements. Eventually his efforts unleashed a raging controversy over public versus private rights to medical research innovations.

Bob's research had been supported by the Crippled Children's Society in the amount of $5,000 per year. The NARC had given him an annual grant of the same amount. In addition, a total of $743,700 of federal money had gone into his program. Bob would have been happy to continue spreading the gospel of PKU screening and working each night into the wee small hours of the morning in his lab developing additional tests, but suddenly with no prior experience with lawyers, he was faced with a whole flock of them.

One bright day in the spring of 1963 a momentous meeting took place at Buffalo Children's Hospital to work out an agreement on the marketing and implementation of the PKU test. In addition to Bob, an attorney for the University of Buffalo was in attendance, as was an attorney for the National Crippled Children's Society and an attorney from a private company that wanted to manufacture and market test kits. Several representatives from the NARC also participated. Bob's main concern was to achieve widespread and efficient use of the test. The outcome of the meeting was that the private company would market the test. Bob did not ask for any remuneration, but it was agreed that the company would donate five percent of its profits to be divided among the NARC Research Fund, the Crippled Children's Society and the University at Buffalo Foundation Incorporated. The price to be charged for the kits was never discussed.

Bob had not patented his invention. Even though a formal invention report had been requested on January 10, 1962, by the Public Health Service, Bob was so preoccupied with overseeing the trial of his test, training representatives of state health departments to perform the test, packaging the test kits and traveling in the U.S. and abroad to publicize the good news that a simple test for PKU had been developed that he had little time or energy left for such administrative details. Almost a year later, after four follow-up letters and numerous phone calls to Bob's lab from the Public Health Service, that agency finally received the invention report.

A patent attorney had been hired by the state university system of New York to work with Bob. He had seemed very helpful, spending a weekend with Bob to go over all the details. Although neither Bob nor the state university system people were aware of it at that time, it was later disclosed that this person was really a patent attorney for the private company. The patent application was filed in Bob's name and shortly thereafter Bob entered into an exclusive licensing agreement with the private company for the life of the patent.

Bob was pleased, thinking that all was well. The test kits would be marketed, five percent of the profits would be divided among agencies that had helped him to develop the test, newborn infants would be protected against PKU and he could go happily back to his laboratory. This turned out to be only the beginning of Bob's troubles.

By the time the company was ready to market the test materials, Bob's laboratory had begun to distribute its own kits for the national trial funded by the Children's Bureau. The private company announced their kits would be marketed at the price of $262 per kit to test 500 babies—over 40 times the cost for Bob's lab to produce these kits—which was six dollars. Bob was appalled by what the company intended to charge. As far as he could tell the only difference between his test kits and those produced by the private company was that the cardboard boxes used by the company to package the kits were stronger than his.

That was when the politicians became involved. The Senate Labor and Public Welfare Committee was soon to report out the Health Research Facilities Bill, a $280 million boost to an expanded National Medical Research Program. Senator Russell B. Long, assistant Senate majority leader, was angry—and eager to report that the Public Health Service had not approved the agreement with the private company, although the two voluntary health associations involved and the Children's Hospital of Buffalo had supported it. Bob Guthrie was criticized for seeking the private marketing of the PKU test kits and because it appeared he had been remiss in carrying out his obligations to the Public Health Service. The senator did admit, however, that Bob would not have made any profit from the arrangement. As Senator Long stated, "In the Guthrie case, neither the university nor the Children's Hospital at Buffalo had the knowledge, the background or the sophistication to know what is, or is not, in the public interest." He added that, "A charge that is 40 times what it cost Dr. Guthrie to produce the kits for field trials, especially when all of the basic development and promotion had already been done, is in my judgment an outrage."

The company involved issued a statement that it had never sold any of the kits for $260, that it had spent thousands of dollars in setting up PKU test manufacturing facilities, and that it was now assembling a unit to test 325 babies which would sell for $67.71.

Senator Long added an amendment to the Health Research Facilities Bill to spell out the government's rights to control marketing of medical innovations or inventions developed with federal aid. The upshot was that ownership of the invention was granted to the United States and no single laboratory was granted exclusive marketing rights. Senator Long acknowledged that Bob Guthrie had coöperated in the end result.

As a result of the Guthrie case, the Public Health Service tightened its patent reporting procedures to require that invention reports be made on federally-supported research projects no later than the date on which research findings were published in journals. The modified Long Amendment permitted the federal government to provide three-year exclusive manufacturing rights to private contractors using medical inventions fully or partly financed with federal funds under certain conditions.

5

Piggyback Testing

Bob Guthrie's involvement with lawyers, patent attorneys and politicians thus ended on a good note. It should be emphasized that Bob never made a dime out of the marketing of the PKU test. If he had been paid one cent for each filter paper used in the test he would have become a wealthy man indeed, but he never asked for that recompense. His goal was to have the test marketed as cheaply as possible so that all children around the world could be protected.

After the success of the PKU test, Bob was anxious to devise tests for other treatable metabolic disorders. He started immediately on a test for galactosemia, a disorder in which an infant is unable to convert the sugar galactose to glucose because of the absence of the enzyme uridyltransferase. Unlike PKU which only causes mental retardation, this can be lethal. Galactose is present in breast milk as well as in cow's milk, so whether an infant with galactosemia is breast-fed or bottle-fed, the galactose builds up in its body and causes physical symptoms such as nausea, vomiting and weight loss. Thus milk, the perfect food for infants, is highly toxic to the rare babies who have galactosemia. It can cause death within a few weeks if not treated; thus a newborn test is of utmost importance.

Like PKU, galactosemia is a recessive genetic condition in which both parents of a galactosemic patient have a defective gene for the disorder. It occurs in one in 50,000 births and is much rarer than PKU. Dr. Ken Paigen, who moored his sailboat near Bob's in Lake Erie, gave Bob the idea for the test. He suggested the use of a mutant of *E. coli* that lacked the same enzyme, uridyltransferase, as did the affected infant, and had its growth inhibited by the disc of blood from such an infant. An infant with galactosemia is unable to convert the sugar, galactose, to glucose because of the absence of uridyltransferase. The basis of a galactose-restricted diet is either soybean milk or a casein hydrolysate, Nutramigen. By 1963 Bob and his staff had developed a dried-blood-spot test for galactosemia as well as one for maple syrup urine disease (MSUD), so named because the urine of the patient smells like maple syrup.

MSUD is another metabolic disorder that causes progressive physical and mental degeneration—and death—if untreated. Like PKU it is inherited recessively, so there is often no documented family history. Although it is a rare disease worldwide, it is found much more frequently (about one in 300) in the Mennonite population due to intermarriage. The mutation was brought to the Mennonite community in Lancaster County, Pennsylvania, some 200 years ago by Klaus Zimmerman, who immigrated from Switzerland. He had 14 children, who in turn had large families, so the mutation was off to a good start in that population. The state of Pennsylvania has recently begun screening for MSUD. The treatment consists of a diet low in the amino acids valine, leucine and isoleucine, which the patient cannot metabolize.

Bob enlisted three laboratories to collaborate with him in his work—the Oregon State Public Health Laboratory, St. Joseph's Hospital Laboratory in Burbank, California, and the Massachusetts Public Health Laboratory. In 1967 Erie County, New York, joined the list of collaborating laboratories. All of these labs had directors who were very interested in newborn screening. With their participation the new tests could be tried out on routine newborn specimens.

Bob had a two-year grant from the Children's Bureau for a trial of the PKU test. This grant was extended until 1968 to cover many of the other tests that were developed in his lab. He called this technique "piggyback testing" as he piggybacked other tests onto the specimen taken for the PKU test. For each additional test he merely punched an additional disc from the dried-blood spot. It was his theory that when a state enacts a mandatory PKU screening law, the groundwork is laid and the machinery is in place for adding other tests. Each additional test should then cost less than a dollar per child. Bob pointed out that with each succeeding test the cost would be cheaper for more rare conditions. This "piggybacking" research led to the process of making a biochemical fingerprint of the infant to identify treatable conditions.

In 1964 when St. Joseph's Hospital Laboratory became a part of Bob Guthrie's collaborative study on testing for PKU, galactosemia and MSUD, a young engineer, Tom Vaalburg, was working for Dr. Ruben Strauss, director of the pathology laboratory. He also worked part-time for a local engineer who has been called an inventive genius, Robert Phillips. Bob Guthrie later referred to him as a very good business man and a humanitarian.

Due to an injury during World War II, Bob Phillips was an amputee and had become intrigued with adapting mechanics to medical technology. Having spent so much time lying in hospital beds in the days before they could be raised and lowered electrically, he saw the need for a bed that a patient could raise or lower without having to summon someone to crank it up or down. After consulting with an orthopedic surgeon, Bob Phillips engineered such a bed in his garage workshop. The patented idea was sold to the Simmons Company and for a period of time, before electric hospital beds became common, these beds filled a very real need.

By 1964 Bob Phillips had started his own company called Fundamental Products. When Tom Vaalburg described to him the laborious process involved in doing the Guthrie test—how the blood discs had to be manually punched out of each sample and placed on agar trays—they began to work on automating the test. By the time Bob Guthrie came to visit the lab at St. Joseph's Hospital, Bob Phillips' punch-index machine was being used there. It automatically punched quarter-inch discs from four different dried-blood spots and placed them on four different agar trays.

Bob Guthrie was amazed and immediately realized the significance of this invention. He asked whether the machine could be adapted to punch four samples from a single blood spot in order to test for four different disorders. The typical specimen was collected on a three-by-five inch card with spaces for the baby's identification to be written at the top and with four half-inch circles at the bottom to be impregnated with the infant's blood. Bob Phillips and Tom Vaalburg made the necessary changes to the card so that with each punch stroke four discs were punched from a single blood spot and then deposited in four different agar trays. With this innovation, which allowed up to 16 specimens to be taken from a single infant card, the punch-index machine became the automation machine of choice for the newborn screening community.

Bob Guthrie immediately bought one of the machines for his lab, one for Oregon and another for Massachusetts. The punch-index machine revolutionized newborn screening and is now used in most states and many other countries.

6

A Son with Mental Retardation

John Guthrie played an important role in this story. Had it not been for his son John, Bob might never have become interested in mental retardation or made his discoveries or wielded such a worldwide influence on behalf of people with mental disabilities. John was born in Washington D.C. in 1947 while Bob was working at the National Institutes of Health in Bethesda, Maryland. Margaret's pregnancy was difficult and her blood pressure rose gradually during the pregnancy. The baby was born two weeks early and it was immediately obvious something was wrong. Johnny cried constantly and was a light sleeper. He did not nurse well as his older brother, Tom had. He was slightly smaller than normal and slow to gain weight. As an infant, he enjoyed rocking and swaying movements, bouncing and rocking his crib so much that it could be heard throughout the house. He enjoyed being spoken to and watching his older brother and music seemed to soothe him. Nuzzling soft toys was a childhood pastime and as an adult he continued to enjoy them. John was slow in attaining the developmental milestones of rolling over, sitting up, creeping and walking. Finally at the age of 16 months he walked, but he never developed clear speech.

Caring for Johnny and two-year-old Tom became increasingly difficult for Margaret. The following summer when Bob and Margaret went home to Minneapolis for their vacation, they consulted a pediatrician who placed Johnny in the hospital, not because he was ill but because Margaret was so exhausted. He thought it would give her some relief. Like many other parents of children with special problems, Bob and Margaret began to search for help for Johnny. They took him to a famous endocrinologist, Dr. Hubert Wilcken at Johns Hopkins Hospital, because John's testes had not descended and their pediatrician believed that this might be a symptom of other endocrine problems. Dr. Wilcken said the testes would descend later, which they did, and that there were no other endocrine problems, but he thought that perhaps Johnny had a hearing loss because he did not turn his head when spoken to, so they took him to the speech and hearing clinic at Johns Hopkins. There he was given a skin test, popular at that time as a hearing test for infants, in which the resistance to electrical current in the skin was checked when the infant was frightened by a sound.

The theory was that if the infant was frightened its skin would sweat and there would be less resistance to electrical current. The diagnosis was made that Johnny had practically no hearing in one ear and very little in the other. Johnny was provided with earphones, which he did not like. This was natural as the diagnosis was wrong. They discovered later he had very good hearing. The problem was that Johnny could not form a conditioned reflex to sound and therefore the hearing test was useless. He continued to develop but at a very slow rate. He liked toy cars and enjoyed his rocking horse. When his new sister, Anne, was born in 1949, he was very interested in her.

In September when Bob took the position as chair of the department of bacteriology at the University of Kansas and the family moved to Lawrence, Margaret enrolled in the Louise Tracy Correspondence Course for Mothers of Deaf Children. She worked with Johnny in matching colors and articles and feeling objects. He loved the special attention but did not make a lot of progress. Margaret also started taking him to Kansas City once a week to a preschool for children with hearing impairments. Margaret describes him at that period as being a little blue-eyed blond boy in high-topped Buster Brown shoes who was small for his age and very curious. He enjoyed running around outside their barrack apartment investigating objects. He also learned to ride a tricycle. Although he attempted to say many words, his speech was still poor, but it soon became obvious that Johnny could hear well.

When the Guthries moved to Staten Island in 1950 there were many neighbor children for John to enjoy watching. He and his younger sister Anne became good friends and he learned a lot from her but it was obvious that he wasn't developing normally. Finally Bob and Margaret took Johnny to a psychiatric clinic where he was diagnosed as having autism. They read all the available literature about autism and felt terribly guilty as this indicated that the parents of children with autism were often cold, intellectual types. Again they took Johnny to Johns Hopkins, this time to see the famous Dr. Leo Kanner who had invented the term "autism." He raised their spirits by saying Johnny did not have autism. However he could not make a diagnosis.

Next Bob and Margaret took Johnny to Dr. Gesell's famous clinic at the Yale University Medical Center where he was given a comprehensive examination. Afterwards the Guthries received a thoughtful letter in which Johnny's brain was compared to a radio set with some damaged circuits. This led them to a well-known pediatric neurologist who told them in a very blunt manner that Johnny was mentally retarded. He suggested that they should be prepared to place him in an institution.

This was an upsetting experience for both Bob and Margaret, mostly due to the brusque manner of the doctor. Instead of looking for a residential facility for Johnny, the couple searched for a day program that would meet his needs and soon found there were only two or three programs in all of New York City for children with developmental disabilities. All were run by Jewish organizations, but none were near their home, so Margaret enrolled him in a local day-care center for children without disabilities. There John was somewhat of a loner, but he copied the other children and participated in some of the activities, climbing, doing simple puzzles and so on. He was particularly attracted to the phonograph and mechanical toys. His speech was still poor, however, and he never answered questions. Anne always rode along with Margaret when she picked him up and she looked forward to playing with the equipment too.

Johnny was somewhat concerned when his sister Barbara was born in the fall of 1951. At first he thought they had traded Anne for the new baby, but soon Anne, Barbara and Johnny became a threesome, tagging along with Margaret for John's various appointments. Later Johnny attended a kindergarten at Wagner College where he did fairly well, although he never developed a special friendship with any other children. He just enjoyed watching them play. Shortly before the Guthries left Staten Island, a parents' group for children with mental retardation was formed and Bob and Margaret attended the first meeting. Bob suggested they name the group "The Staten Island Aid for the Mentally Retarded" and the name was adopted.

When Bob and Margaret moved to Williamsville, New York, in 1954, Johnny was thrilled to watch the moving van. Their new house was on a street with lots of children for him to watch at play as he rode his trike up and down the sidewalk. He loved going on rides at Glen Park and playing house with Anne and Barbara. His older brother Tom remained Johnny's role model; he wanted to be big just like him.

As soon as Bob and Margaret were settled in Williamsville, they took Johnny to the rehabilitation center at the Children's Hospital. Dr. Robert Warner headed the program and later it was he who got Bob involved in PKU research. Although Johnny was seen by many professionals at the center, no one was ever able to diagnose his problem. They tried every test imaginable. They tested his urine and his blood for metabolic conditions and found that his problem was not metabolic. They checked his chromosomes, which were normal. It was just a condition the family had to live with without knowing the reason why.

Johnny was now seven years old, attending a private school in Buffalo run by the Erie County chapter of the New York State Association for Retarded Children, for there was no program for children with developmental disabilities in the local public schools. Bob became quite active in that organization, serving as vice president and later as president. Bob also became active in the Williamsville PTA and attended the school board meetings. Finally he and Margaret and the parents of the three other local children with mental retardation met with the superintendent of the Williamsville School District, Mr. Keller, about the transportation problem. He told them the state of New York would compensate a school district that provided transportation for their children since there were no special classes in the suburban schools. The school board members then decided that if they could provide transportation to football games for their nonhandicapped students, they could certainly provide transportation to a private school for the children with disabilities.

Eventually in 1957 a special class was set up at the local Academy School for children with developmental disabilities in Williamsville. One Buffalo suburb had reported that no children with mental handicaps resided there. However, after this class was started, parents of several children in that district requested admission for their children.

In 1956 another brother, Jim, was born. Grandma Guthrie visited often and was very concerned about Johnny. She prayed that he would recover. Johnny had one friend, Doug, who would come to the yard and call for him. Johnny was like the other children in a number of ways. He had several record players which needed many repairs. He contracted all of the childhood diseases such as measles and chicken pox. And he was no trouble for baby sitters. An early riser who enjoyed his breakfast, he liked to play doctor, dentist and psychologist scribbling "reports" and "prescriptions" on many sheets of paper. He learned to ride a two-wheel bicycle without much trouble. When Robert and Margaret moved their family in 1958 to a larger home in which they stayed until 1995 Johnny missed his friends, although the new house was only a few blocks away from the old one. Perhaps some consolation was the birth of his youngest sister Patty.

A few years later when John was ten, he began attending a special class at the Academy School directly across the street from their home. He never mixed well with the other children, but he learned about the community. Reading was impossible, but he mastered his colors and could set the table. At home many stuffed animals had taken up residence on his bed. Records were still a favorite, especially The Beatles, The Monkees and The Mommas and the Poppas. Some TV programs like Zorro and Popeye held his attention. He was fascinated with the movie *The Wizard of Oz* and talked a lot about Dorothy. He even liked girls named Dorothy. A favorite neighbor he called his "fat, juicy girl" came visiting one day. Johnny got so excited he fell over his wagon and broke his arm. He had always been attracted to overweight people. When the family drove back to Minnesota for summer vacation, John loved camping. Water pumps and toilets or outhouses were targets of his investigation at each camp ground.

John finished the Academy Street School when he was 15 years old. His last teacher had been excellent, teaching him some cooking and allowing him to do some cleaning in the school cafeteria. From there John moved to Sweet Home Junior High School in 1962 where he stayed until 1965. His teacher, Anne Ragoven, worked hard with him on reading with flash cards and he did very well with her. She was dedicated to her kids and wrote a book, *Learning by Doing,* while John was in her class. He posed for many of the pictures that appeared in the book. She has since published several other books. John was very fond of Ms. Ragoven, who thought he might be ready for vocational rehabilitation. Even so, she recommended he attend the high school special program until he was 21 years old.

John did many of the things nonhandicapped boys did as teenagers. He took swimming lessons for a couple of years and learned the basic strokes. He joined a Cub Scout troop for boys with disabilities and attended Cub Pack meetings at the school each month. Later he was welcomed into a Boy Scout troop at the Methodist Church where the boys wore the Scout uniforms. Several of the Eagle Scouts helped the boys in his troop learn some of the Scout oaths and work toward merit badges. During two or three summers John attended a camp in northern Pennsylvania staying a week at a time and doing very well.

Bowling was great fun for John. He was one of the original members of a bowling league for the mentally challenged which started with five or six people and eventually grew to 50 or 60 people. They bowled twice a month, celebrated Christmas and end-of-the-year parties together and received trophies and other favors. For 25 years he participated in that league and enjoyed it very much. He also attended a Bible study class each week.

From 1965 to 1968 John attended special classes at the Williamsville South High School. With some shop work and part of each day spent cleaning at the Academy School, he still acquired a few academic skills. He learned about money and time and for a while attended BOCES (Board of Coöperative Educational Services) classes where he was trained in food service. During that period his parents were involved with a social club for teenagers with handicaps. All of the parents took turns planning Friday evening social events like movies, plays or miniature golf. In 1968 John graduated from high school in a special BOCES ceremony. He was 21 years old.

John, Margaret and Bob Guthrie (l. to r.)

7

Encounters

It was June 20th, the day the Guthries were to leave for their summer vacation visiting their relatives in Minnesota. The whole neighborhood was excited. The VW van with the boat tied on top was parked in the driveway. Tom and Jim were helping Bob attach the trailer. They had intended to start early but as usual their plans had gone awry. As the morning wore on they were still packing. Margaret stowed groceries in the compartment Bob had built at the back of the trailer for a kitchen. Toward noon the neighbor children came over to wave goodbye, but the family was not quite ready. Finally at six p.m. they started on their way and the neighborhood heaved a sigh of relief. Bob and Margaret had decided they were going to leave on June 20 and they were going to do it, even if they only drove 20 miles that night.

The younger children went to sleep as they rode. It was exciting to ride at night and not know where they would be in the morning. Finally Bob pulled into a camp ground, Margaret helped him set up the tent and they went to sleep. In the morning Johnny was the first one awake and out of bed to explore the camp, checking out the toilets so he could report back to his family whether they were flushers or pits.

The thousand-mile trip to Minnesota usually took four days out of their two-week vacation. They had numerous flat tires and a few breakdowns. On one trip the car developed engine trouble before they even got out of Buffalo. When there were no mechanical difficulties, the children would devise plots for stopping progress. Once Bob had screeched to a halt because there was a turtle in the road. After that whenever anyone yelled, "Turtle in the road," it signaled it was time to stop for ice cream cones.

In Minneapolis in addition to Grandma Flagstad there were many cousins to visit. Grandma Guthrie lived at Lake Minnetonka where they enjoyed swimming and boating, just as Bob had done when he was young. Before 1958 these vacation trips were the only time when Bob completely relaxed. There was no laboratory keeping him busy half the night so he devoted himself to doing as little as possible. All too soon the two weeks would come to an end and it would be time for the family to pack up their van, put the boat back on top, stow their equipment in the trailer and head back to Buffalo.

After 1958, the year that Bob moved to the department of pediatrics at Children's Hospital in Buffalo, these vacation trips became less relaxing. As a result of his new job Bob became reacquainted with people in the department of pediatrics at the University of Minnesota where researchers in PKU began to collect urine specimens from untreated children with PKU for Bob to take back to Buffalo with him. In his research he isolated a substance in the urine of untreated individuals with PKU which he called the TA factor. The substance turned out to be betaine, a discovery which led him to publish a few short papers on the subject.

Although Bob Guthrie's development of the PKU test opened up the possibility for his lab to develop tests for diagnosing many other treatable disorders using the same dried-blood spot technique, he would have been the first to admit that he could not have achieved these accomplishments without the help of many loyal people who were inspired by his vision and were equally dedicated to preventing mental retardation and developmental disabilities. Many of the people he hired—from lab technicians to researchers to secretaries—

remained with him for years and came to feel like members of an extended family.

In 1956 Mrs. Ada Susi was the first of those to come and stay. She had been a nurse in her native Estonia and had served as head operating room nurse in a hospital in Iowa before coming to New York State. Licensing regulations kept her from working as a nurse in New York so she accepted the position as Bob's head technician and was his closest assistant for many years. Mrs. Sally Bloom arrived that same year and became the coördinator of Bob's program. Sally began as a volunteer with the National Society for Jewish Women. Bob remembered how the women from this society would come and park their cars in front of the little house belonging to the NARC where Johnny first went to school when he was seven. They would work as aides, helping in numerous ways and then drive home again in the afternoon.

Sally was particularly interested in Bob's program and finally agreed to give up her volunteer status to become his full-time coördinator. In fact she became so involved that although her own children did not have mental handicaps she joined the Erie County chapter of the Association for Retarded Citizens, an organization made up mainly of parents of children with mental retardation. Eventually she became an officer and served as vice president during the time Bob was president of the organization. As time went on Sally worked in nearly every phase of Bob's program, collecting urine specimens, helping with the writing of research papers, even becoming involved in the control of grants and money management. One thing she swore she would never do was take blood samples. However she ended up doing just that and became an expert in the procedure. Eventually she developed a screening program in the Dominican Republic with funds from the Variety Club. Recently Sally expressed regret that Bob never got a lifetime stipend for his research. She felt that he was charismatic and overly generous. According to Sally, "Bob [could] stand in front of an auditorium full of people, wearing a hand-me-down suit, one red sock and one blue one, and in two minutes have everyone in the palm of his hand."

Another employee, Mrs. Joan Edwards, became Bob's administrative assistant when Sally Bloom retired. Joan first became acquainted with Bob because her son had mental handicaps. In 1979 because of Bob's "dunning" she and two other women rode with him to the first state conference on the prevention of mental retardation. Awestruck in his presence, she took 60 pages of notes on that ride. Like most of the people who have worked with Bob over the years, she is fiercely loyal to his accomplishments and feels proud to have been part of the team that since 1964 tested more than 300 million children around the world for PKU, preventing more than 27,000 cases of mental retardation. In her years of working with Bob she found him to be thoughtful and generous.

In May 1980 Joan helped coördinate a prevention conference in Buffalo attended by 300 people from all over the U.S. As a result, the Western New York Task Force on Prevention of Mental Retardation and Developmental Disabilities was formed. A year later they incorporated and Joan Edwards became the executive director. At first she received no salary and used the sun porch of her home as her office. Now she has federal and state funding and a staff of five.

Among other noteworthy employees is Dr. Michael Garrick, hired in 1970. At Bob's suggestion he began doing research to develop a test for sickle cell disease using a dried-blood spot. As part of his research he was attempting to convert fetal hemoglobin to adult hemoglobin in goats and when he joined Bob's team he brought a herd of goats with him. Bob's challenge was to find a farm for the Goat Brigade. In his work Dr. Garrick bled the goats but never hurt them. In fact he was very fond of them and had pictures of them on the walls of his lab. He ultimately developed a dried-blood spot test for sickle cell disease which was introduced in New York as part of the state program in 1976, years before it was used anywhere else.

Dr. William Murphey came to Bob's lab in 1966. He was intrigued by inborn errors of metabolism and ten years later he moved to Oregon where one of his main contributions was the introduction of testing for congenital hypothyroidism in the United States, a test already in use in Canada. By placing an ad in *Science* magazine Bob found and hired Dr. Edwin Naylor, an expert in genetic screening who remained with Bob for 13 years. Soon after this, Dr. Tom Paul joined the team. Tom had earned a Ph.D. in biochemical genetics and he and Ed Naylor designed the labs at Acheson Hall. Later Tom left to attend law school in Houston. Another long-time employee, Kathi Hilbert, started as a glassware washer in Bob's lab when she was 21. Eventually she became his secretary and remained with him for 20 years.

Most of the people Bob hired over the years were stable and hard-working, but he found, to his chagrin, that in at least two cases he made serious misjudgments in character. Around 1950 Bob hired an attractive young Chinese woman (we'll call her Lee) through the employment office at Sloan Kettering Institute. She worked hard and was extremely loyal. Among lab personnel she was jokingly called "The Bank of China" because she lived frugally, rarely using her pay checks. Anyone who was short on cash could always borrow from her.

Bob realized that there was a problem when she began to repeat her experiments over and over, saying they weren't good enough. Bob felt they were fine. Then he learned that she had been a graduate student at Harvard University, that she had done most of the work for her Ph.D. and had been writing her thesis when she suddenly quit. Bob had a visit from Lee's sister who told him that Lee suffered from schizophrenia. Her sister had her committed to an institution. Later Lee wrote some rather strange letters to Bob saying that she had to get going again. She was released from the institution and visited Bob on one occasion. It was obvious to him that she was on some sort of medication. She never again pursued her scientific career.

Later Bob hired as a post-doctoral fellow a man who had been older than most when he got his Ph.D. (We'll call him David.) He came with good recommendations and seemed quite capable. Bob knew that he suffered from schizophrenia and had been in an institution on Long Island, but he was on tranquilizers and worked well at first. Occasionally David would forget to take his medication which led him to believe that everyone else was crazy. He thought that somebody was sabotaging his experiments by doing things to his incubator, but Bob knew this to be untrue. Eventually David stopped taking his medication altogether, became more and more paranoid and then stopped coming to work. Concerned that he was suicidal, Bob got a court order to allow him and a detective to break into David's house. David was then committed to a psychiatric institute in Buffalo.

This episode was not without its benefits for Bob's research in PKU. While David was in the institution Bob was able to arrange for one of his technicians to set up a laboratory in the institution. With David's help all the residents there were checked for PKU. Among the 2,000 residents tested, one was diagnosed with PKU. That person had a sister in Pennsylvania with PKU—and she had three children with severe mental handicaps because she had not been on diet during her pregnancies.

While he was working for Bob, David completed some work on *Escherichia Coli* and wrote a paper which was accepted and published by the *Journal of Bacteriology.* He was later released from the institution, but again quit taking his medication and applied for jobs in other places. Unsuccessful in finding work he wrote letters to the dean of the medical school blaming Bob for his inability to find employment. David was married and had a family. Bob often talked with his wife about him, but eventually they divorced and Bob lost contact with the family.

After the test for PKU was developed, there was a great deal of interest in starting programs across the country. Bob was often asked to speak at meetings on the subject of screening, and this involved a lot of traveling across the United States. In addition he was already quite active in the Association for Retarded Children. Over the years he was involved in the organization of 25 conferences on the prevention of mental retardation and developmental disabilities. For several years he used an exhibit on the topic of prevention entitled "The NARC-AAMD-PCMR Working Together." In efforts to get the Canadian and the U.S. associations for the mentally handicapped to work more closely together, Bob added meetings in Canada to his well-filled agenda. This led to his traveling abroad in the 1960s as international organizations began forming to prevent mental retardation worldwide.

Bob's first European meeting was an international gathering in London in 1960. That was the beginning of the International Association for the Scientific Study of Mental Deficiency (IASSMD) which continues to meet every four years. He also became involved in the International League of Societies for Persons With Mental Deficiency (ILSPMD). That organization represented more than 100 countries where parents' groups had been established. In 1962 Bob provided an exhibit at the International Association of Pediatrics in Lisbon that included handing out boxes containing the materials to do the PKU tests. At that meeting Bob learned something that is now common knowledge among professionals working with persons with PKU: the low-phenylalanine diet can be helpful even for people who have been diagnosed too late to prevent mental retardation. Dr. Carl Ashley, the Maternal Child Health Director at Portland, Oregon, presented a paper reporting the beneficial effects of the diet on teenage boys who had never been treated. Their hyperactivity and autistic-type behavior improved markedly when they received the diet. One boy was able to leave an institution and work in his father's butcher shop because of the improvement in his behavior.

One of the people who picked up Bob's materials in Lisbon was Dr. Doreen Murphey, a pediatrician from Ireland. Upon her return home she reported to Dr. Seamus Cahalane, an influential physician in Dublin, who found that the test worked very well. Because of Dr. Cahalane's influence, the Republic of Ireland became the first nation to do the test country-wide. Dr. Cahalane discovered that in Ireland

PKU has a frequency of one in 5,000—the highest in the world except for Turkey. Using tests developed in Bob's lab he also diagnosed a case of galactosemia, one of MSUD and one of homocystinuria. Needless to say, Seamus Cahalane became a strong advocate for screening and attended every international meeting until he retired. Bob and Seamus Cahalane became good friends and on a subsequent occasion the Guthries camped in Dr. Cahalane's backyard during their round-the-world trip.

Following the meeting in Lisbon, Bob was taken on a wild ride in a VW across Portugal and Spain to Madrid where he was to catch a train for France. The young driver who had offered Bob the ride made the trip at breakneck speed, with Bob occasionally sticking his head through the open sunroof to take snapshots. Despite all of his efforts, the train had already departed when they arrived at the Madrid station. Bob had to settle for a seat atop his luggage between cars on a later train. At that time a civil war was raging in Spain and Bob found himself sharing his cramped quarters with numerous soldiers.

In some countries it was the parents' groups that were instrumental in getting screening accepted as a routine medical procedure. In Scotland a parents' association for children with disabilities sponsored visits from Dr. Jim Farquhar and Dr. John Scott, who gave many talks and generated enough interest to start newborn screening in that country. In England screening was initiated by Dr. Joseph Ireland, a biochemist in Liverpool who read a paragraph in an English journal saying Dr. Guthrie had devised a method for blood phenylalanine estimation. After Dr. Ireland wrote to Bob and received in return an outline of his methods, he and his colleague Dr. E. G. Hall, a pathologist, began using the Guthrie method in the laboratory.

Dr. Hall had a problem getting permission to take blood samples and proceeded to do the tests on urine. As a result Dr. Ireland found five treatable PKU cases in 1958. These children were attended by Dr. Anne MacCandless, a pediatrician. Later on, Dr. Freddie

Hudson, another pioneer in the PKU field, took over their care. In addition he kept a register of all PKU children born in England. After his untimely death, this register was maintained by Dr. Isabell Smith at the Hospital for Sick Children in London. Bob Phillips' punch-index machine never came into use in England as Dr. Bob Kennedy of Scotland had invented a machine of his own which was used there and in England. Eventually there were approximately 30 different screening programs in England; unfortunately all of them were very small.

In 1965 Bob spent nine weeks traveling around the world spreading the gospel about newborn screening. His trip was paid for by so-called "480 money". This was money that had been loaned to other countries by the United States during World War II which was to be used for projects of mutual interest after the war. It was made available due to Congressional Act number 480, thus the title "480 money". So Bob was invited to India to talk about neonatal screening for PKU, visiting many other countries along the way. His first stop was Geneva, Switzerland, where he visited Dr. Gunnar Dybwad and his wife Rosemary who were working for the International Union of Child Welfare. In Gunnar's work, visiting other countries in Europe in his little VW car, he had taken along two movies about newborn screening. He found the car to be the easiest method of getting them across borders, so while performing his duties he was also promoting Bob's test.

Every place Bob went he set up a little folding exhibit with hand-out materials about the test. Rosemary Dybwad had even arranged a meeting for him on his way to India with people in Teheran, Iran. Since he had only a six-hour layover between planes, he held his meeting in a hotel lobby near the airport where he set up his exhibit and put out some literature. In New Delhi when he talked about neonatal screening, he found the Indian pediatricians were interested in child health but, probably due to the myriad of other problems in that country, they did not seem interested in screening. To this day screening is not being done in India.

67

From India he continued on to Tokyo for an International Pediatrics Association meeting where he was hosted by Dr. Hiroshi Naruse and Dr. Teruo Kitigawa. Bob had arranged to hire a Japanese secretary who spoke English to help with his exhibit. An attractive young woman who had gone to English school in Tokyo, she had read all of the literature for the exhibit ahead of time and was able to describe the test for the Japanese doctors. She was also an excellent dancer, allowing Bob to enjoy the social as well as the work aspects of the meeting.

These travels were not without complications. On that same 'round-the-world trip Bob inadvertently left his flight bag containing two cameras in India. His decision to purchase new cameras for himself and Margaret set into motion the "Japanese Camera Caper." Bob's secretary took him shopping in Tokyo where he bought a new camera for Margaret, a string of pearls and a lovely new camera for himself. The situation became complicated when one of Bob's colleagues, representing the U.S. in research in Asia, arrived in Tokyo with Bob's flight bag. It had been sent through the embassy in India to the embassy in Tokyo. Suddenly Bob was overwhelmed by a great abundance of cameras. He was able to return Margaret's camera to the store. However a customs form had already been completed for the camera he had bought for himself and it could not be returned. Fortunately one of Bob's friends agreed to take it off of his hands when he got home.

Despite all of the apparent interest, PKU screening did not become common practice in Japan until nearly ten years later due to opposition from obstetricians. But this introduction to Japan had an impact on Bob and he returned on many more visits. The people were generous and hospitable, and he made many lifelong friends among the Japanese professionals with whom he had contact. Bob later became a consultant to the Japanese newborn screening program but found that they did not really need his services. The Japanese screening personnel were particularly hard-working and coöperative.

Australia and New Zealand were also on the itinerary for that 1965 trip. Bob was especially enchanted with New Zealand, its people and fantastic scenery. He visited with some health personnel who had written him in the early 1960s—Joan Mackay, director of maternal and child health for the country and Dr. Donald Beasley, later to become president of the International League. Dr. Beasley worked in Whangarei, 100 miles north of Auckland, and he was dedicated to the prevention of mental retardation. When Bob wrote he would like to visit him on his round-the-world tour. Dr. Beasley responded that he was only a pediatrician in a small town, but Bob persisted. Dr. Beasley met him at the airport in his second-hand Jaguar and took him to the meeting he had arranged. Bob showed a movie, set up an exhibit and did a slide show for an audience of three people, but as Bob said, "They were all the important people." Bob was impressed and so were the people from Whangarei.

While in New Zealand, Bob also met with Dr. Arthur Veale, newly returned from England where he had earned a Ph.D. in genetics. Intrigued by Bob's work, Dr. Veale was attempting to set up a program in which a number of hospitals in New Zealand would do the test. Dr. Veale and Bob quickly became close friends and colleagues.

Physicians were beginning to screen for other disorders in addition to PKU. Dr. Tsagaraki of Greece had come to Bob's lab in the early 1960s to learn about screening. She began a screening program in 1965 at the Institute of Child Health, but her work was halted because of a military junta and she was unable to continue until the junta was replaced by a democracy. Her screening program was for both PKU and G-6-PD deficiency, the latter condition occurring frequently in Greece and causing a disease called favism, a term derived from the fava bean. Fava beans, common in Greece, contain a substance that produces the effect of lysing (destroying) the red blood cells in affected people. It is a hereditary disorder in which the enzyme G-6-PD is deficient in red blood cells and is passed on through the X chromosome; thus the disorder is found only in boys.

Those children who have this condition become anemic and sometimes die if they eat fava beans. Screening for this disorder is essential in Greece.

One of the early international meetings on inborn errors of metabolism was held in 1967 in Dubrovnik, Yugoslavia—again financed by 480 funds. At that time there was still a controversy over the real value of the PKU diet, whether or not the seeming improvement of the patients was due to a placebo effect. Much of the discussion focused on that question. At a meeting in 1969 in Heidelberg arranged by Dr. Horst Bickel the main topic was congenital hypothyroid screening. This was followed by an international meeting in Tel Aviv. The discussion continued at both places about the efficacy of the diet. An interesting note was made at the Tel Aviv meeting that in Israel there were few positive results from the PKU test. Drs. Szeinberg and Ben Cohen did follow-up work in Israel and found that some Ashkenazi Jews are mildly hyperphenylalanemic. However the occurrence of classical PKU is almost nonexistent among Ashkenazi Jews.

One of the people most committed to screening in the whole of Europe was Dr. Otto Thalhammer of Austria. Bob met him in 1971 at an international meeting and later visited his lab. Dr. Thalhammer was not only doing about nine tests that had been developed in Bob's lab, he had also invented a foot-operated punch to facilitate the testing process and was hiring students from the university to do all of the punching of the discs for the test plates. Thus his technicians were relieved of the laborious, routine work. Bob was impressed by Dr. Thalhammer's work and was able to make a suggestion, based on improvements made by Karl Susi in his own lab which made the operation of picking up the discs and placing them on the test plates more efficient. He used a little bent copper tube attached to a vacuum. Dr. Thalhammer gave Bob one of his punch machines to take to China along with a note to the Chinese people saying, "From the smallest country in the world to the largest country in the world. Best luck for screening."

In Stockholm Bob visited Dr. Hans Palmstierna who had spent some time at Bob's lab in Buffalo learning about the test. He had returned to Sweden determined to organize screening in that country, but then had become involved in environmental matters so did not expand newborn screening as much as he could have. He wrote a regular newspaper column for the country's political opposition party and a book he wrote about the environment was translated into several languages. Dr. Palmstierna drowned several years later ending a remarkable life.

In Poland Bob visited Dr. Barbara Cabalska, who had come to his lab in Buffalo when his assistants were first demonstrating the test, and then she and Dr. Nina Duczynska, a biochemist, had started newborn screening in Poland in the late 1960s. Bob visited their lab in 1971 and was surprised to find that their research staff was composed almost entirely of women. He learned that at that time the Polish government had passed a law allowing no more than 50 percent of the medical students to be women because it appeared that medicine was becoming a feminine profession. Bob was impressed by the fact that the walls of the lab were covered with pictures of children who had been treated for PKU, enabling the technicians to see the results of their work. Dr. Cabalska had initially screened only one fifth of the country. There was not enough money for the diet product in the rest of Poland since they did not produce the product there and had to pay for the imported product with dollars. Neither could she afford a punch-index machine. Eventually she procured one of Dr. Thalhammer's pedal-operated machines. Because of Dr. Cabalska's interest an international screening meeting was held in Poland in 1972—again supported by 480 money.

In 1975 Bob was invited back to Japan for another meeting and found that since his last visit a nationwide screening program had been organized there. Japan had about 50 of Bob Phillips' punch-index machines and eventually the Japanese became the best customers for these machines. The technicians demonstrated the tests, pouring the agar plates and running the punch-index machines. The meeting was very well organized and Bob felt he really did not have much to do. He decided that his main function was to have his picture taken, as there were many people there with cameras asking him to pose with them for snapshots.

Bob returned to Tokyo in 1982 for the fifth international meeting. Again it was a successful meeting supported by the federal Japanese government, industry, obstetricians, pediatricians and parents' groups, convincing Bob that the Japanese had the best national newborn screening program in the world. Although the programs in New York or Oregon are equally good, Japan's is nationwide with federal funding in addition to support from many private organizations. Even their previously recalcitrant obstetricians are now in support of newborn screening.

On one of his visits to Japan Bob gave a talk for the Society of Little Pigeons, an organization for the parents of children with Down syndrome—which was also supporting newborn screening. Watching the 300 people at the meeting, Bob was in awe of their organization and the energy invested in the event. The explanations on all of his slides had been translated into Japanese ahead of time and there was always an interpreter at hand. Of course his lecture took twice as long as it would have in the U.S. because the translation was not simultaneous, but that did not seem to bore the audience. After the lecture he was presented with a little pigeon lapel pin. On another trip Bob gave a speech sponsored by a large newspaper in Tokyo— with 500 people in attendance. Over the years Bob was awarded some lovely gifts by the people of Japan—including a Pentax automatic camera that was not yet on the market in the U.S. and a model ship that he had greatly admired, which traveled home in his lap on the plane so that it would not be damaged.

Bob gleaned an interesting fact regarding the practice of medicine in Japan. They wanted to include the test for congenital hypothyroidism in the newborn screening program because it could be done with the same blood specimen used for the PKU test, but they refused to use the radioimmuno assay, the test used in the U.S., because their federal government would not support anything having to do with radioactivity.

The southern hemisphere was on Bob's itinerary in 1984 when he attended an international congress on clinical chemistry in Brazil. Dr. Rosemary Dybwad arranged for him to meet enroute with members of UNPADE, a parents' group in Santiago, Chile. Dr. Marta Colombo in the Institution of Nutrition at the University of Chile wanted to know more about screening for PKU as she had personal knowledge of 70 cases that had gone untreated. Dr. Colombo was aided by Dr. Erna Raimann, a pediatrician who specialized in urea cycle defects and other metabolic conditions of children. Veronica Cornejo, a nutritionist, became interested for personal reasons. Her sister had a baby with PKU who unfortunately was diagnosed too late for the diet to have any effect in preventing mental retardation. Due to the efforts of these people, screening was begun in Chile.

Bob's crusade was carried to other countries in Latin America. He visited Dr. Antonio Velazquez, a graduate of the University of Mexico Medical School who then earned a Ph.D. in human genetics in Michigan. He often wrote to Bob asking for current articles. Upon his return to Mexico he began a screening program in his own lab, which was run by his father, a retired pathologist. PKU, MSUD, homocystinuria and galactosemia were all tested in this program—without the luxury of a punch-index machine. Eventually Bob Phillips drove to Mexico with one in his car to avoid trouble with customs.

Another Latin American country that is starting programs to screen for PKU and maple syrup urine disease is Costa Rica where Dr. de Cespedes has clinically found ten cases of MSUD and now that he is screening will undoubtedly find additional cases. Bob always felt that the incidence of MSUD was probably higher in Latin American countries where there is an increased population of descendants of Spaniards. In Spain the frequency of MSUD is four times higher than in other countries. Dr. Jiminez, another contact in Costa Rica, was involved in studying iron deficiency. He showed that severe iron deficiency in infants results in later developmental delay that cannot be corrected by prescribing iron for it is an irreversible process; however, if treatment is instituted immediately, it is effective and simple. Bob realized that the test he had been using for detecting lead poisoning could also be used to detect iron deficiency.

In 1984 Bob also visited China where a screening program had recently begun, mainly due to the influence of Dr. Rui Chen who had spent two years in Los Angeles where he was associated with Drs. Richard Koch, Kenneth Shaw and George Donnell studying inborn errors of metabolism. When he returned to the Shanghai Institute for Pediatric Research he began screening under the director Dr. Guo Di who was very supportive of Dr. Chen's efforts. Bob spent ten days on the mainland: eight days in Shanghai and two days in Beijing. He stopped first in Tokyo to meet with a group of pediatricians who were supportive of the screening program in China. Dr. Kitigawa had spent several days in China and had sent Bob a long report on the situation there. Bob carried with him a supply of Lofenalac because Rui Chen had been unable to make or procure the product in China. Although Bob had been able to carry the supply free on Canadian Pacific Airlines, upon his departure from Tokyo the Japanese airline charged him $100 for overweight freight. He considered this ironic as it was the Japanese pediatricians who were trying to help China with screening. The products he carried were from the PKU parents' associations in the U.S. and Japan. Some diet products were later sent from the Milupa Company in Germany.

In Shanghai Bob found a very active program in operation. It was regionalized, with all specimens coming to one laboratory. They had already diagnosed four cases and although it was difficult to get the diet product in China, all four cases were being treated. In the northern part of the country where screening was being done they had found 15 cases of PKU. Early figures indicated that the frequency was about one in 15,000, almost what it is in the U.S.; however, not enough cases had been found at that point to make that estimate statistically valid.

While he was in Beijing Bob met a remarkable person, Zuo Chi Hua. Without federal support this woman in her 60s had arranged for more than 20 different hospitals to send representatives to a course she taught on PKU and screening. As a result 121 hospitals had begun to screen and had found eleven cases of PKU. Only two of the cases could be treated as the diet was unavailable in China. These two were treated because their pediatrician worked for a year with a pediatrician in Japan who sent him the product. Rui Chen has concentrated on the diet problem and it appears that he has finally succeeded in getting a pharmaceutical company in Shanghai to produce a phenylalanine-free product.

After China Bob's next stop was Taiwan, but the political situation made it impossible for him to fly directly there from mainland China. The airport employees in China would not even attach luggage tags for Taiwan, so Bob was forced to fly to Hong Kong and change planes there. Officials went with him through the transit area in Hong Kong where the luggage tags were changed. Security was so tight that one could not use a camera or binoculars on the plane. Upon arriving in Taiwan, Bob's luggage was inspected by the customs officials who promptly discovered that he was carrying a bag that was marked in large letters, "Shanghai, China." Inside were some international newspapers from his Shanghai hotel room. An irate customs official pulled the papers out of the bag, threw them on the floor and said in a very loud voice, "Communist newspaper." That was Bob's introduction to Taiwan.

There was a tremendous contrast between this island and mainland China. In China the only cars he saw on the roads belonged to an embassy or were owned by a business or corporation and the streets were crowded with people, buses, street cars and bicycles. Bob noticed that soldiers, even police officers, were unarmed. Soldiers working beside the road were planting trees. He could not help wishing that soldiers in the U.S. could be kept busy planting trees. In contrast he had never seen as many guns in his life as he saw in Taiwan. Not only were police officers and soldiers armed, but high school students marched on the street in military fashion. Everyone seemed preoccupied with the fact that mainland China was only 100 miles away—and there were cars everywhere.

In Taiwan Bob's host was another Dr. Chen, also interested in screening for PKU in spite of the fact that the frequency of PKU is very low among the 18 million people from southern China who have settled in Taiwan. Bob suspected that the frequency of PKU was also low in southern China and that G-6-PD deficiency would be much more frequent so he put Dr. Chen in touch with Dr. Sophia Tsagaraki in Greece so she could share her experience in screening for G-6-PD deficiency.

Unusual experiences seemed to plague Bob on some of his travels. After one trip to Japan in 1985 he continued on to Australia and New Zealand. Customs agents in Sydney stopped him when they found his films about PKU testing. Apparently they were very nervous about the possibility of pornographic films entering the country. The agents informed him they would have to screen the films before he could bring them into the country and the screening would take place the following Tuesday. Bob's schedule allowed only a six-hour layover in Sydney before he was to catch a flight to Brisbane for a five-day tour. Fortunately Dr. Elizabeth Anderson, head of a local department of pediatrics, had sat next to Bob on the plane. She immediately intervened, explaining what the films were about and who Bob Guthrie was. The customs agents relented and Bob was on his way.

For a few days in Melbourne Bob was the guest of Dr. David Pitt, who had introduced PKU screening there. He explained that when they had first started screening in Perth, they could not convince the Aborigines to give blood samples so urine specimens were used instead. A technician held up two agar plates for him to see. On one were dark red dried-blood specimens; on the other were white discs from the Aborigines. Bob also discovered that Dr. Brian Turner of Sydney had started screening infants at four weeks of age with urine specimens because he could not get the hospitals to coöperate in getting the blood spots from the newborns. Later, of course, they converted to the blood screening. In Adelaide in 1985 Bob met Dr. Neil Wigg, who was involved in research that demonstrated prenatally and postnatally the effect of low levels of lead on the IQ.

These trips were not all business. On one occasion in Sydney he was lured into going surfing. As he paddled out to sea on a borrowed board, he suddenly realized that the water was very quiet and all the other surfers were far behind him. Remembering that sharks hunt in those still waters, he quickly paddled back to shore and that was the end of his surfing career.

Bob was impressed by the yacht clubs in Sydney. He found there were 52 yacht clubs there because boating was so popular, and on one occasion Bob was asked if he'd like to crew in a sailing race. Of course our sailor accepted. The boat was a 22 footer made of fiberglass and the race was to last more than three hours. There were 22 boats in this race, but Bob found to his surprise there were many sailboat races going on simultaneously. It seemed the larger boats had the right-of-way, or at least they took the right-of-way with shouts of "Get out of the way, you bloody fools!" Bob's job as number four crew was to remain in the companionway and take lots of pictures. His boat came in third.

On a later visit to Sydney Bob spent time with Dr. Bridget Wilcken, a researcher in metabolic disorders, and with Dr. Gillian Turner, known worldwide for her work on chromosomes and her important pioneering work on the Fragile X syndrome. Dr. Wilcken had demonstrated how important it is to screen for cystic fibrosis. Each infant born in New South Wales, Australia, is now screened for this disorder. However, there is a long way to go before cystic fibrosis screening is done in the U.S. The only states doing it so far are Colorado and Wisconsin.

Dr. David Wilcken, Bridget's husband, a professor of cardiovascular medicine, discussed with Bob his interest in familial hypercholesterolemia. This is a dominant condition in contrast to the other disorders Bob had studied. Dr. Wilcken's idea was to screen babies to find families in which there is a need for treatment and clinical follow-up for this condition. Eventually Dr. Wilcken got a grant from the Australia Heart Association to begin this screening. In 1985 Bob met again with Dr. Joan Mackay, director of the maternal and child health, whom he had known for 20 years. And on all of his trips to New Zealand he visited his good friend, Dr. Arthur Veale.

The sixth international PKU meeting took place in 1986 in Austin, Texas—the first to be held in the U.S. Dr. David Wilcken attended and shared some of the first results of newborn screening for hypercholesterolemia in New South Wales. He called this test "reverse screening" because he was screening babies to find families in which adults needed clinical attention because of the risk of early heart attack or stroke.

Bob met Dr. Benjamin J. Schmidt from São Paulo, Brazil, in 1972 at a meeting in Montreal. Subsequently Dr. Schmidt visited Bob's lab while Bob was away and learned about the test from Ada Susi. Dr. Schmidt was remarkably successful in getting screening started in Brazil because he was able to persuade APAE (the Association of Parents and Friends of the Mentally Handicapped) of São Paulo of its importance. This association is a private institution and was the first one in Brazil to perform newborn screening for PKU and hypothyroidism on a population basis. When Bob visited Dr. Schmidt in São Paulo in 1986, he found that Dr. Schmidt had been able to get five states in Brazil to pass laws mandating newborn screening for PKU and hypothyroidism. In the meantime, a federal law was passed extending the obligation to the whole country. Brazil was the first country outside the U.S. to pass such laws. (Every industrialized country in the world except the U.S. and South Africa has socialized medicine so such laws are not necessary.)

Dr. Schmidt speaks several languages and is a talented organizer. He was the president of the International Pediatric Association (IPA) for five years and helped turn the APAE newborn screening laboratory into the one with the largest volume of specimens in the world; in 1986 it was processing 40,000 specimens per month. In the late 1970s Dr. Schmidt reported finding a baby with both classical PKU and congenital hypothyroidism. The latter has an approximate incidence of one in 5,000 worldwide. The chance of a baby having both conditions would be about one in 50 million. In 1988 São Paulo hosted the seventh international screening symposium sponsored by APAE-São Paulo where Dr. Claud LaBerge presented information about a new test for congenital hypothyroidism that was being developed on dried blood spots.

Through Dr. Ricardo Guell, whom they had met at that São Paulo meeting, Bob and Dr. Naruse were invited to participate in a three-day program on perinatal diagnosis in Havana, Cuba, in 1989. Knowing nothing about Cuba before his arrival Bob found their screening program to be impressive. It was the first country he had visited where neonatal screening was begun by testing for sickle cell disease. Later tests were added for congenital hypothyroidism and PKU. Every pregnant woman is screened for sickle cell disease, alpha feto-protein and AIDS. In addition more than half the population is screened for HIV virus. Those who are found to be positive are placed in a sanitorium to protect the general population from the virus.

After Bob retired he gave up some of his traveling and speaking engagements; however he continued to take an active interest in screening programs and attended as many meetings as possible. In 1990 he went to an international meeting in Paris, and another in Auckland, New Zealand in 1991 with an auxiliary meeting in Sydney, Australia, dedicated to the memory of Dr. Arthur Veale. At these last two meetings Bob encountered many of his former colleagues met during his sabbatical leave in New Zealand.

With each contact made, Bob's enthusiasm for newborn screening was reproduced many times. His influence grew stronger as more and more people learned of the marvelous possibilities for prevention that this technique offered.

John Gerrard, Evelyn Hickmans and Horst Bickel, (l. to r.), pioneers who developed the first low-phenylalanine formula.

Gunnar and Rosemary Dybwad and Bob, early advocates of PKU testing.

8

Waging War on Childhood Lead Poisoning

In the late 1960s due to the urging of his friend Dr. Robert Mac-Cready, who had been so enthusiastic about screening for PKU, Bob Guthrie turned a portion of his energies toward the prevention of childhood lead poisoning. "Why worry about lead?" his colleagues might have asked. Only in the last few years has the medical community become aware of the insidious danger of lead poisoning, for once lead is in a person's system, it is deposited in the organs and not excreted. In addition it interferes with the ability of red blood cells to carry oxygen, thus inhibiting the ability of all organs (including the brain) to function normally. Lead can only be removed by a process called chelation in which a chemical is injected into the body that combines with the lead so that it can be excreted in the urine.

As late as 1975 when Bob was a consultant to the California Department of Health, he tried to arouse interest in childhood lead poisoning. One dedicated professor of pediatrics, otherwise committed to the prevention of developmental disabilities, tried to dissuade him saying, "Bob, I've never seen a case of childhood lead poisoning in California in my life." Bob's response was, "How do you know that you've never seen a case?" The professor had never thought of it that way.

During that same year Bob got a call from the director of Sonoma State Hospital, an institution for the mentally retarded. There was a serious problem of lead poisoning among the residents. The hospital staff members observed those residents with high lead levels and found that they were tearing the pages out of magazines and chewing them. The inks from the colored pictures were especially high in lead and that was being swallowed and absorbed through the gastrointestinal tract.

Lead has been a blessing and a curse for centuries. It was the first metal ever worked and is also the oldest pollutant known to humankind. By conducting a lead analysis of the bones, anthropologists and archaeologists are able to identify the social status of an individual whose thousand-year-old skeleton has been extracted from a dig. The higher the lead content, the more likely it was that they used lead cooking utensils, a sure sign of a higher social status.. Well-to-do Roman citizens also suffered from lead poisoning because the pipes carrying their drinking water were made of lead. In addition Romans had the habit of drinking heated wine from lead goblets. Although there is no proof, it is considered likely that lead poisoning was one of the major causes of the decline of the Roman Empire. Lead did not come into wide usage in the modern world until the invention of the internal combustion engine. In the early 1920s there was considerable controversy in the United States over the possibility of introducing tetraethyl lead into gasoline. At first it was considered "God's gift" to American life by General Motors as it would improve the efficiency of the automobile engine, even though it was considered a threat to public health by other leading figures.

To settle the controversy, a commission was appointed to look into the matter. According to an article in the *Journal of Public Health* in April, 1985, it seems the chair of this commission had been paid by either Dupont Laboratories or General Motors to influence the commission's finding—which found in favor of adding lead to gasoline. The auto industry boomed and with the advent of the industrial revolution, increasing amounts of lead were unleashed in the environment. By the 1940s lead was detected in glacial ice. Industrialized society has now been deluged with lead. In addition to its use in gasoline, lead is used in the manufacture of batteries and has been a boon to the paint industry. Most of the paint produced before World War II, and some quantities since then, contain lead. In fact it has been authoritatively estimated that more than 30 million housing units in this country are hazardous to children because of leaded paint. It would cost well over 100 billion dollars to remove this hazard. Even the glaze on some pottery contains lead that can leach into food and be ingested. Some pottery factories in the U.S. have been closed in recent years because of lead pollution of their grounds.

Most physicians can recognize serious lead poisoning in children, since the child suffers from vomiting, convulsions, mental retardation, paralysis, and, in severe cases, death. At lower levels, however, it is more difficult to establish the effects of lead poisoning. Studies have found that symptoms such as hyperactivity, learning disabilities, low achievement in school, behavior problems and mental retardation can also be traced to lead poisoning.

A classic publication in 1979 by Dr. Needleman and his associates, who analyzed the lead level in several hundred baby teeth, found that the IQ of children with high lead levels was four points lower at the mean of the distribution curve than that of children with low lead levels. This small difference in the mean would correspond to a much greater number with mental retardation and also far fewer gifted children at the extremes of the distribution curve. Dr. Needleman was able to talk the children into giving their baby teeth to him rather than leaving them for the tooth fairy by giving them each a button with a picture of a tooth on it saying, "I Gave."

Lead is everywhere. It enters the body through different routes. Babies and small children put everything into their mouths. They munch peeling leaded paint. They chew on their crib rails and toys which at one time were painted with leaded paint. The dust near main highways is loaded with lead from auto exhaust. Children play in the dirt, suck their fingers and absorb additional lead. Bob's own father had worked in a lead mine near Marionville in southwestern Missouri as a young man. Lumps of galena are easily dug out of the soil. In countries such as Jamaica there are backyard battery factories where batteries from cars are reconditioned. Children learn that the lead battery terminals taste sweet when sucked.

In the mid-1960s Bob asked his colleagues Dr. Bill Murphey and Mr. Adam Orfanos to develop a lead test using a dried-blood spot. They were never able to develop such a test but they did begin testing for free erythrocytic protoporphyrin (FEP) which is a precursor of heme, the red substance in blood hemoglobin. They simplified this test which had been developed by Dr. Sergio Piomelli who had used it on a dried-blood spot. While the test does not directly analyze the lead level, it was a way of measuring the effects of lead since lead interferes with the ability of the blood to form hemoglobin. A simple test for lead poisoning has yet to be developed.

Dr. Emma Kay Harrod, a deputy commissioner of the department of health for Erie County, New York, and an early proponent of lead testing, provided the first blood samples to start the program. Not only were these samples used by the researchers in Bob's lab to modify the FEP test, making it more practical, but they were also used by a colleague, Dr. Michael Garrick, who was doing research on a newborn test for sickle cell disease. Surprisingly they identified one child who had both sickle cell disease and lead poisoning—bad luck both genetically and environmentally.

The testing program was small at first as there was no federal money available. The first federal money was a six-million-dollar grant obtained in 1972 by Congressional action from appropriated funds that had been impounded by President Nixon. The money was distributed in small amounts throughout the country. Later the federal Center for Disease Control (CDC) began funding lead screening programs.

As Bob became increasingly interested in the problem of childhood lead poisoning, he found that the government had been slow to recognize the danger of this pollutant. For years the Center for Disease Control set the official cutoff level (the maximum level at which blood lead was not considered to be harmful) at 30 mcg per 100 ml of blood. Since then the CDC has continually reduced that standard to its current level of ten mg. If Bob had had his way the standard would be zero since this toxic substance has no known positive role to play in the health of any animal species.

It would seem that the reduction of lead in gasoline during the 1970s came about because of the realization on the part of the medical community and the government of the threat to health posed by lead. This was not the case. It was to protect the health of the catalytic converter installed in all new cars to reduce other pollutants in the engine exhaust. Indeed during the early days of the Reagan administration it became known that the Environmental Protection Agency, under the direction of Anne Gorsuch, was planning to relax the regulations and again allow more lead content in gasoline. This fact was leaked to the news media, creating a great outcry in 1982. This was understandable because the article by Dr. Needleman and his associates had appeared in the *New England Journal of Medicine* in 1979 showing that exposure to lead in early childhood was causing the lowering of the IQ in children.

A national health survey called NHANES II was carried out from 1976 to 1980. Blood lead was one of the substances measured. Of the 65,000 individuals surveyed, 10,000 children six months to five years of age were included. Much to everyone's astonishment, four percent of these children were found to have blood lead levels over 30 mg per 100 ml, the accepted cutoff at that time. This survey also found that there was a reduction in the average blood lead level that paralleled the reduction in the use of leaded gasoline nationally. These new facts and the resulting publicity brought about the Reagan administration ruling that levels of lead in gasoline should be lowered. In fact this was the only environmental protection regulation that occurred during the Reagan administration. Also by the time this ruling was announced, a new director had been appointed to the EPA.

More recently it has been found that blood lead levels slightly higher than we all currently carry as members of modern urban society can irreversibly damage a child's later development whether the child is exposed before or after birth. This is the conclusion of three large studies in Boston, Cincinnati and South Australia. The Boston study is based on the work of Dr. Needleman and his associates, who measured cord-blood lead levels on 12,000 newborn infants and published the results. Lead had been absorbed in utero by some of the infants. Dr. Bellinger, a Massachusetts scientist, followed up with those children and found that a significantly larger number of those with high lead levels were now in special classes in school because of learning problems. Dr. Needleman also followed up with the children (now high-school-aged youth) whose teeth he had studied in 1979. He found an increased number of high-school drop-outs in the high lead group.

In the lead poisoning research begun in Bob's lab by Dr. Murphey and Mr. Orfanos in the early 1970s, dried-blood-spot specimens were obtained from residents of the West Seneca Developmental Disability Center in the suburbs of Buffalo. Many of these individuals had recently been transferred from the Newark Institution for the Mentally Retarded. Higher elevations in the FEP were found in many of the specimens from residents recently transferred. Bob contacted the pathologist at Newark, but before Bob had time to explain the reason for the call, the pathologist said he felt they had a lead problem. He had found "basic stippling" (a sign of lead poisoning) in red blood cell smears seen under the microscope in his lab.

When the matter was investigated it was found that lead-based paint had been used in the Newark Institution. In fact as Dr. Murphey had predicted large quantities of lead-based paint had been purchased by the state and stored long before there were laws against its use in the interiors of homes in this country. Shortly after that Bob's lab screened some of the institutions for people with mental handicaps in the Canadian province of Ontario and found serious problems in at least two facilities. A year later Bob mailed the results and copies of some of the correspondence to the administrator of all New York State institutions. As a result most of the state facilities were screened and steps taken to correct the problems.

Because of Bob's involvement in the National Association for Retarded Children he became acquainted with two young brothers who were leaders in the Youth National Association for Retarded Children. They became interested in the problem of childhood lead poisoning and developed screening programs funded by the Knights of Columbus aimed at small towns in southern Illinois. They were able to enlist the help of voluntary organizations and during the summer they screened preschool children, mailing the dried-blood specimens on filter paper to Bob's lab, which processed about 5,000 specimens for them the first year, after which they processed their own FEP tests. Their results were enlightening. When they began their efforts they met resistance from local health authorities who informed them that there was no lead poisoning problem in southern Illinois. Such problems were found only in places like Chicago. After screening they discovered that about five percent of the children tested had lead levels above 30 mcg per 100 ml of blood.

In the mid 1970s Bob organized a serious effort to screen preschool children in the suburbs and rural areas of upstate New York using the FEP test. This continued over a period of years, eventually leading to the testing of nearly 50,000 specimens. Bob's lab personnel were assisted each year by two premedical students who worked full-time as lab technicians. Of the 47,230 children tested they found that more than one in 200 needed further testing, reporting back as having blood lead levels of over 30 mcg per 100 ml. Their research found that one-and-a-half percent of the suburban and rural children had either lead poisoning or iron deficiency. While many people assume there is no problem with lead in the suburbs, this research showed that lead poisoning is not just an inner-city affliction.

Perhaps Bob's most interesting work on lead poisoning occurred when he lectured at an international meeting in Toronto in 1982. A pediatrician from Kuwait, Dr. Azza Shaltout, told Bob she suspected a serious lead poisoning problem in her country. As a result Bob provided her with the filter papers for the FEP test and in a three-year period his laboratory screened over a thousand dried-blood-spot specimens that she sent from Kuwait. The results confirmed Dr. Shaltout's suspicion. Some of the samples had the highest FEP levels Bob had ever seen. Seriously elevated lead levels were found in 66 percent of the randomly selected samples obtained from a Kuwaiti hospital emergency department. Five infants' blood lead levels were so high they needed immediate treatment; one eight-month-old infant died of acute lead encephalopathy.

Some 198 additional samples were sent to Bob's lab from healthy children at a well-baby clinic in Kuwait and 36 percent of those children had elevated FEP levels. Drs. Shaltout and Guthrie concluded from the frighteningly high incidence of elevated lead in the small number of children tested, and especially among supposedly healthy children, there was a serious epidemic of lead poisoning in Kuwait. Dr. Shaltout believed that the practice among the Arab women of using black eyeliner, kohl, was the source of the problem. In Arabic countries women, even little girls, customarily wear heavy eye make-up. This is especially important to women in countries where many of them are still veiled. Their eyes are the only facial features visible to the outside world and they must be beautiful. Kohl did indeed make their eyes look beautiful. They seemed to sparkle, as if mirrored by tiny diamonds. When the kohl was analyzed much of it was found to have a very high lead content. In fact much of it was prepared by grinding up lumps of galena (lead ore) or lead sulfide. This product was inexpensive and the tiny platelets of galena produced the beautiful sparkle. This use of eye makeup was a part of their culture that had been practiced for generations.

In 1984 after the study had been completed, Bob and Margaret traveled to Kuwait at the invitation of Dr. Shaltout. Bob and Dr. Shaltout met with government authorities to discuss the problem. X-ray photographs taken of many of the infants in Kuwait reveal "lead lines" which indicated that the lead in the kohl had been absorbed by the mothers and deposited in the bones of their unborn babies. This fact is now well-known in Kuwait and photographs of these lead lines have been published in the *Journal of Tropical Pediatrics.*

Not until 1985 did Bob hear of the suggestion from Dr. Gillian Turner of Sydney, Australia, that if a woman is exposed to lead as a young child, the lead will go to her bones and stay there until she is of child-bearing age. Then when she becomes pregnant the lead will be brought from her bones to her fetus by the same enzymes and support systems that transport calcium from a woman's skeleton to the fetus. This suggestion has proven to be true and there are probably more than a million women in the U.S. alone who are currently affected in this way.

The Kuwaiti government reported that the children poisoned by kohl came from Saudi Arabia, Syria, Iraq and from Bedouin populations as well as from Kuwait. The following year Bob visited Kuwait on his way to a meeting in India where he was to report on his experience with lead poisoning. He met again with Dr. Shaltout along with several government health authorities. As a result of this meeting, the Kuwaiti government banned the use of galena in kohl. They also developed a lead-testing program and a lead clinic which operated at least until the invasion of Kuwait by Iraq in 1991. However this program may not have been particularly effective, as Kuwait is a wealthy sheikdom in which only one in three of the people are Kuwaitis. Although government money is used for public health and education, many rural women shop in country-side markets where there is little control or government supervision. Bob lost contact with Dr. Shaltout after the war, but it is hoped the program is still functioning.

When Bob arrived at the international meeting in New Delhi, he reported on his study of lead in Kuwait and learned that this practice of using a lead-based eyeliner, called *surma* in that part of the world, was common there and undoubtedly in Pakistan and Bangladesh. A pediatrician in Bombay announced he had analyzed eight

consecutive samples of *surma* and found a lead sulfide content vary-
ing from 20 to 80 percent. The *surma* is applied to the conjunctiva or
inner surfaces of the eyelids, making it easily absorbed into the system. It is also ingested by hand-to-mouth activity and through the
skin as it is also applied to the eyes and sometimes to the navels of
newborn infants, on some occasions as often as three times a day. It
is often mixed with menthol, causing the eyes to water, and stimulat-
ing children to rub their eyes. Thus lead enters their systems through
their tear ducts. Women of these countries who wear kohl or *surma*
from the cradle to the grave are thus poisoned before they are born.

Bob was convinced little knowledge regarding the extent of this
problem existed in Asian or Arabic countries and could find no survey to indicate how extensive the use of lead-based eyeliner is. He
found only three medical journal articles between 1978 and 1981 that
discussed lead contamination among Moslems from the use of
cosmetics. The Middle Eastern health authorities did not seem to
have been alerted to the problem as the articles were obscure, with
Kuwait being the only exception. Even though lead has been banned
in kohl in Kuwait, controlling its distribution remains difficult. It
continues to be cheap and easily obtained, especially by the tribal
people who get it from local "healers" and marketplaces rather than
from modern retail stores. Government action is a slow process,
especially in such heavily populated countries as India and Pakistan.

This problem, discovered in the Middle East, has traveled closer to home for roughly 800,000 Pakistanis, East Indians, Arabs and
other Middle Eastern people reside in the U.S. A million Pakistanis and Indians live in England. The use of black eyeliner is tradi-
tional among these people, and it was Bob's feeling that there are
frightening implications to this widespread problem. The average
IQ in the countries affected could be seriously reduced, producing
a population with a lowered ability to improve their social conditions. Scientific, educational and cultural contributions and achievements could also be affected. Bruce S. Kershner concludes in *Kohl*,
"It is possible that the behavioral problems caused by lead poison-

ing, if extensive enough, could affect the political stability of an already unstable region."

In 1984 Bob Guthrie traveled around the world to learn more about what was being done to address childhood lead poisoning. In London very little lead screening was done, although work had been done on the problem in other parts of the country. In some towns in Scotland water is still carried in lead pipes, but rather than replace the plumbing, these towns found a cheaper alternative. They were able to lower the lead levels in the water by liming the pipes. The acidity of the water was then reversed and lead was no longer leeched out of the pipes.

From this point on, Bob Guthrie crusaded against lead poisoning, wearing a large lapel pin that read "Get the Lead Out;" however he did not pursue lead screening any more. The FEP test does not actually measure the amount of lead in the blood and his lab was not equipped to do actual lead screening. In recent years there has been more recognition of the importance of lead poisoning in modern industrialized society so lead levels are falling and the FEP test is not accurate with the lower levels of lead. It was heartening to Bob that lead was finally being recognized as an insidious, dangerous poison, permanently damaging the minds and central nervous systems of our precious children.

Bob Guthrie, Crusader

9

The Guthries on Trek

Late one June afternoon in 1968 a new VW camper pulled out of the Guthries' driveway with Bob at the wheel, Margaret beside him and Johnny in the back seat. It was followed by a green and white VW station wagon driven by Barbara with Anne beside her as navigator, Jim and Patty in the back and a moped tied on the front. This was no ordinary vacation trip to Minnesota. It was the beginning of Bob's leave-of-absence. The family was off on the first leg of a journey that would take them to New Zealand after a zig-zag trek across the U.S. and through parts of Canada.

After all of the publicity that resulted from the development of the PKU test, Bob had been in demand as a speaker all over the world. Eager to spread the gospel about PKU screening, he had traveled to the corners of the earth in his tireless efforts to inspire converts. His one regret was that he could not afford to take his wife or children on any of these adventures.

His visit to New Zealand in 1965 had been particularly memorable for it was in Wellington that he had met Dr. Joan Mackay and her husband Ian. They had immediately fallen under his missionary zeal regarding PKU screening as had Dr. Donald Beasley, his pediatrician friend with the used white Jaguar in the town of Whangarei on the north island. Back at home Bob was determined to take a year's leave-of-absence in 1968 and take his family with him to a foreign country. With all of his recent contacts, New Zealand seemed to be the ideal place. An English-speaking country would pose no language problem for the children. Bob had been impressed with the physical beauty of the country and the fact that sailing was a popular sport was a big plus. In addition it would give Bob an opportunity to set up a screening program for the Islands of the Pacific, something he had dreamed of doing since his 1965 visit. Then in 1967 Dr. Mackay had visited Bob and Margaret at their home in Buffalo while she was on a World Health Organization fellowship. As they discussed Bob's proposal of screening the Islands of the Pacific, Dr. Mackay was enthusiastic. She and Bob were also intrigued by the possibility that the island populations might include some recessive conditions because of consanguinity (intermarriage with relatives). By the end of her visit it was settled: the Guthries would come to New Zealand.

Bob arranged a paid leave-of-absence and Dr. Beasley was able to get the Intellectually Handicapped Children's Society (IHC), the main parents' group in New Zealand, to pay transportation costs for the family. The plan was for Bob to spend his time in New Zealand working with Dr. David Beecroft, but it was later discovered that Dr. Beecroft would be in the U.S. for six months of that year. At that point Professor Arthur Veale notified Joan Mackay that he would be interested in collaborating with Bob.

The trip had to be planned in infinite detail. The whole family was going, plus Tom's bride Mary. That made nine Guthries. After much discussion, they decided to travel by ship—the cheapest transportation for a large family. Tom and Mary were in the state of Washington planning an August wedding, so the family was organized to travel across country in two VW buses to the northwest where the bride and groom would join them. They would continue down the coast to California where they and their two vehicles would board a ship for New Zealand.

One VW was already in the family garage—a reliable second-hand station wagon. In addition they purchased a brand new VW

camper that could be used for sleeping space at night. It had a sliding door on one side and it was the first VW camper in the city of
Buffalo. In fact the VW agency wanted to keep it for a while for a
display at the convention center, but the Guthries couldn't wait. Bob
felt that it was wise to use VWs because they could be repaired anywhere in the world. He planned to make this a landmark trip.

In anticipation of complaints of boredom from Jim and Patty,
aged ten and twelve, during the 7,000-mile drive across country, Bob
made the back of the station wagon into a game room by turning
the middle seat around to face backward. A small chest of drawers
was placed between the middle and back seats for their games and
belongings and an ironing board lay between the two seats to use as
a game table. Everyone had a sleeping bag and each person had a
duffel bag and a drawer for personal belongings. To save money they
planned to camp across the country. At night the three teenagers
slept in the station wagon. Jim's bed was in the top of the camper
and a cot was placed across the front seat for Patty. Margaret and
Bob slept on a fold-out bed. Bob had built some wooden shelves in
the back of the station wagon for storage space. It was hard to decide
what miscellaneous items would be needed for a year's stay away
from home, but they did take Anne's guitar, a pair of skis, some ten-
nis rackets and a moped that Bob had used for his commute to Children's Hospital. The skis were used once in New Zealand. The ten-
nis rackets were never used. Bob eventually gave the moped away
because it could not climb the hills in Dunedin, the Guthries' home
for nine months.

On the first night away from Buffalo they camped just across
the Niagara River in Canada. Friends and relatives offered respite
along the way, often letting the Guthries camp in their backyards.
Of course they lingered in Minneapolis where Bob built a green box
that sat on the roof rack of the camper to carry the seven duffel bags.
Everything went smoothly at first. Bob had purchased a CB (citizen's band) radio for each vehicle which turned out to be an excellent provision. Anne could consult her maps and call ahead to Bob

and Margaret, letting them know what to expect, when they were going to stop and where they were going to camp. They planned to drive 1,000 miles a week making the trip in seven weeks.

In Minot, North Dakota, they spent a few days with Margaret's brother and his seven children. The 12 cousins had a great time swimming and playing together and the family got some good news and some bad news. The bad news was that the station wagon Barbara had been driving had developed a major mechanical problem and Bob was advised that for such a long trip it would be best to buy a new car. The good news (that arrived by letter) was that a $2,000 per year grant Bob had been receiving from the NARC and the Crippled Children's Guild, which he expected to be cancelled during his stay in New Zealand, would be continued! This meant that with the trade-in for the old station wagon they could afford to buy a brand-new VW bus for $2,500.

The next challenge was to convince Barbara that it was not disloyal to leave the old station wagon in Minot. She refused to move out of the old car. It was not until each member of the family had had a long talk with her that she finally relented. They needed to have her approval on the deal because she was an important member of the driving team, even though she had earned her drivers' license only a few weeks before the trip. The VW salesman was so surprised that a teenage girl would prefer an old green and white station wagon to a brand-new red van that he took a Polaroid picture of her sitting in the old car and gave it to her to carry in her wallet. After Barbara consented, the caravan continued with excess baggage and the moped in a large roof rack on top of the new van.

The children had never been west of Minnesota, so enjoyed driving through the Black Hills and the Badlands of South Dakota and were fascinated by the "little people" (prairie dogs) sitting beside their holes on the plains. Of course they had to stop in Cody, Wyoming, and take pictures of the statue of Buffalo Bill. Yellowstone was a "must" and they spent several days there. Warned not to feed the bears they took precautions, but one night they heard something banging around their ice chest—obviously a bear! Wisely they did not challenge it and stayed in their beds. Morning light proved the bear had indeed forced their ice chest open and taken all the food—plus all the penicillin capsules brought along for Johnny's frequent respiratory infections. Bob wondered what the bear's blood penicillin level was, certain there would be one healthy bear in Yellowstone that summer.

From Yellowstone the family went north to Alberta, Canada, visiting some of Bob's cousins. Going through Waterton Lakes National Park on the Canadian side, they returned to the U.S. and Glacier National Park where they stayed for five days. Then on the first of August the Guthries made camp at Squill Chuck Park in Washington. This was Tom and Mary's wedding day. They left one van in camp and rode together to Wenatchee where Bob rented a motel room so everyone could shower and change from camping gear into their wedding finery and set off for the church in the 100+ degree August weather. The wedding was lovely even though the church was not air-conditioned. Afterwards the entire family was invited to Mary's parents' home for a swim. When Tom and Mary left for their honeymoon, the rest of the family drove on to Seattle and then down the west coast to California. Bob had made reservations on a P&O (Pacific and Orient) ship for the voyage to New Zealand. Tom and Mary were to board the ship in Vancouver after their honeymoon while the others would join them when the ship reached Los Angeles.

In Southern California the Guthries enjoyed beach camping and Disneyland, of course. Bob had a business meeting at the Childrens Hospital of Los Angeles with Dr. George Donnell, a specialist in galactosemia, another metabolic disorder of interest to Bob. He also met with Mr. Bob Phillips, the inventor of the punch-index machine, who planned to send a representative to Europe to sell the idea to the people there involved in newborn screening. He had given Bob Guthrie one of the machines to take with him to New Zealand. Before Tom Guthrie had gotten married he had spent a month with Bob Phillips learning all about the punch-index machine so he could be of some help with it in New Zealand. Although the idea of sending an agent to Europe seemed impractical and premature to Bob Guthrie at that time, later the punch-index machine did indeed revolutionize newborn screening.

The last day in Los Angeles the Guthries spent storing all their belongings in the two VWs, except those items they would need on the ship. The punch-index machine presented a problem. If it was in a separate crate, Bob would have to pay extra freight on it as he had to with the moped. In addition, the customs people would have had many questions that would have been difficult to answer. No one knew what a punch-index machine was. In fact despite Bob's tireless efforts, not many people knew what PKU was. The solution was to bolt the box to the back of the red VW and hope no one would notice it. Bob also had a problem with the roof rack on top of the red van. It was too big. If he had crated it, he would have had to pay $90 extra to ship it. Anything that took up extra space cost extra money. Bob ended up splitting the rack in half with a hack saw and putting it inside the red van. The family's last night in the United States was spent in a motel near the harbor.

August 15th was the big day. The P&O ship came into the harbor and the Guthries boarded and found Tom and Mary safely ensconced in their stateroom. Bob and Margaret also had a stateroom while the five children shared a room. This was to be home for two weeks. These were not first-class accommodations so the rooms were all below the water level with no portholes. The lack of a view did not matter to the Guthries as no one stayed in the staterooms during the day except Johnny. He enjoyed listening to records on his battery-operated phonograph, but he also liked sitting on deck with Margaret watching the swimming and other activities and having cokes in the lounge. The engine room and the bridge fascinated Johnny, who for years afterward played "ship"—making announcements he had heard while under way. When the ship stopped in Hawaii there was barely enough time for a sightseeing tour in the vicinity of Honolulu. This was a disappointment to Jimmy who had dreamed of surfing there and to Johnny who had hoped to see an erupting volcano.

Much of his time on board Bob spent learning celestial navigation. Margaret had given him a plastic sextant for his birthday and he had charts of the Pacific Ocean. He enlisted the aid of Jimmy to help him shoot the sun each day at noon so he could compare his sight with that of the ship's navigator. This procedure took at least half an hour and Jimmy soon found better things to do. Bob then turned to Patty, but before long neither of his children could be found at noontime. Bob kept track of the latitude as well. He had a book of sailing directions for the South Pacific published in the 1930s but until this trip he had never had the opportunity to use it. In the ship's library Bob found a book called *Tinkerbell*, the story of a small-boat voyage across the Atlantic undertaken by a man from Cleveland in a 13-foot boat. Bob thought it was an especially appropriate place to find such a book.

The ship docked for a day at Suva, capital of the Fiji Islands, giving the family time for sightseeing. Meanwhile Bob visited the medical school at the University of the South Pacific spending the day with the principal. He was called the principal rather than dean because the graduates of the school did not get M.D. degrees. They were from islands all over the Pacific and graduated after six years of study when they were obligated to go back to their home islands. They spent the first year learning English so they could read the textbooks. New Zealand was the only country that accepted them for postgraduate study. This raised Bob's hopes that he could get the coöperation of the Pacific Islands in newborn screening. While they were there Bob bought two little TV sets, one for Tom and Mary and one for the rest of the family. He also acquired a few other electrical appliances they would need for setting up their household in New Zealand for he had been told that it was much cheaper to buy things in Suva than in New Zealand.

Finally on September 15, 1968—springtime in New Zealand—the ship landed at Auckland and the Guthries disembarked, punch-index machine, moped and all. They were met by a welcoming party that included Dr. Donald Beasley, Bob's friend from Whangarei, and Dr. Arthur Veale, the only qualified geneticist in New Zealand, who was to become a good friend and colleague. The family was treated like visiting royalty. Bob felt reassured that this adventure would be a rewarding one for the entire family.

New Zealand is an agricultural country consisting of two large volcanic islands covering an area the size of California. It has a population of 70 million sheep and 3 million people. There are many small islands nearby. The Guthries' home was to be in Dunedin on the south island so everything had to be transported there by ferry. They set up housekeeping in a little yellow house at York Place. Bob's work was arranged in advance, but the others had to find their niches. Bob tried to get Barbara to enroll in school, but she objected and he relented as the school year was nearly over. She and Anne first got jobs cleaning floors in a hospital. Later in the summer they packed fruit in the interior of the south island. They sent the family the cast-offs and those "rejects" were the best fruit the family had ever tasted.

Jimmy and Patty did go to school. They were curious about what the children in New Zealand would be like and they discovered that their classmates were equally curious about them. Jimmy went to a boys' school a distance from home and was required to wear a uniform. Johnny promptly started calling him "the Uniform School Kid." On the other hand Patty didn't have to wear a uniform and her school was near the house. On the first day she realized that everyone was staring at her. She was the tallest girl in Standard Four (fifth grade). They measured her and then teased her about her height, but she was soon accepted and welcomed. She was a good athlete and everyone wanted her on their cricket team. Jimmy was also athletic and had no trouble fitting in at school.

There was no cafeteria at Patty's school and the children ordered box lunches, but she missed peanut butter and hot dogs. Stopping at the Cadbury candy store on her way home from school each day was a treat—and she thought the pens at her school were great. You just dipped the pen in ink and pulled on a little gadget that would suck the ink right into the pen. Fountain pens were completely new to her, but that is what they were using in Dunedin in 1968. There were other surprises. Jimmy was impressed that they had corporal punishment. He would talk about the teacher giving some boy "six of the best," which meant six whacks with a ruler. Hymns were also sung in school because there is no separation of church and state in New Zealand.

Johnny probably benefitted more from the stay in New Zealand than any other member of the family. He was 21 years old and had finished the work-study program in the Williamsville school district. In Dunedin he attended an excellent sheltered workshop. Bob found that New Zealand had a workshop system far better than anything then available in the Buffalo area. There was a workshop in every metropolis, even villages.

These were so well organized that even people who lived on isolated sheep stations were brought in by bus Sunday night, stayed the week and then returned home on the weekend. Johnny walked down the hill each morning to a prearranged corner where he was picked up by the executive director of the local workshop. Bob felt the workshops responded very well to the needs of their clients. He met one young man who did nothing but chop wood. That was the only thing he could do, so they developed a program for him. He made kindling which the workshop could easily sell, as nearly every home had a fireplace.

Tom and Mary rented a large house at Sawyers Bay just north of Dunedin for eight dollars a week. It had room for a ping-pong table and came equipped with goats and a flock of chickens. Tom and Mary used the green camper while the rest of the family used the red one. Tom got a position as a chemist at the cannery. Mary had hoped to find a teaching position as she was well qualified but she was not successful in her search. She and Anne ended up working temporarily at a plant that made fountain pens. At Christmastime Tom and Mary returned home to the United States.

Bob's respect for Dr. Arthur Veale increased the more they became acquainted. He was an amazing person and his untimely death in 1987 was a great loss to science. Dr. Veale had finished medical school in the late 1950s and had done a residency in surgery. He then became interested in a rare, inherited disorder called multiple polyposis which led him to decide to become a geneticist. When he inquired about the requirements, he was told he would have to know a lot of mathematics because population genetics was important in the field. He was married at the time and had a child, but he went back to the University of Otago in Dunedin where he studied math for two years. This was followed by a fellowship with Sir Lionel Penrose, a well-known geneticist in England. The Veale family traveled to England on a ship where Arthur was employed as the ship's doctor. He spent four years there while he earned his Ph.D. In 1964 he returned to New Zealand as a geneticist—the only one in the country. He also became a cytogeneticist specializing in studying disorders involving the chromosomes such as Down syndrome.

When Arthur Veale heard that Bob Guthrie was coming to New Zealand, he proceeded to learn everything he could about biochemical genetics and he became very good at it. He was probably the only person Bob ever knew who was knowledgeable about all of human genetics, cytogenetics and biochemical genetics. Ultimately Dr. Veale became a specialist in inborn errors of metabolism and screening. Arthur knew Bob was bringing a punch-index machine and was anxious to learn to use it, so as soon as Bob arrived in Dunedin and unbolted the punch-index machine from the VW, he, Arthur and Dr. Ian Houston set up a screening lab at the medical school. Bob's son Tom helped them get started, but Arthur quickly mastered the machine and Tom had to make only one visit to the lab. Arthur Veale enjoyed competing with the technicians to see how quickly they could set up the plates for the machine. He was always faster than any of them.

By 1969 Dr. Veale was screening all of New Zealand. Eventually he was also receiving 10,000 specimens from the Pacific Islands. There was not a great deal for Bob to do in the lab because Arthur Veale and his technicians did all of the work on the screening project. Because he arrived toward the end of the New Zealand academic year and left in the middle of the following academic year, Bob did not have any regular classes to teach, although he did give occasional lectures. Since the Intellectually Handicapped Children's Society had made it possible for him to be there, Bob gave talks at literally every IHC chapter in New Zealand from Invercargill at the extreme south of the south island to Whangarei in the north of the north island.

With no lab to work in at night, Bob spent most evenings at home with his family. He never had time to watch TV in Buffalo, but in New Zealand he became a fan of *Star Trek*. TV in New Zealand had its advantages and its disadvantages. There were no arguments about what to watch as there was only one channel in Dunedin. Even though there was no color TV, the good part was there were no commercials. When Captain Kirk was about to get killed, or something exciting was going to happen, there would merely be a pause where a commercial would be shown in the U.S. Bob enjoyed the pause as much as anything else. The family grew to appreciate British and Australian programs that were new to them. Most of all, watching TV was a pleasant whole family activity, especially for the children who had rarely had their father at home before. Barbara remembers it as a turning point in her relationship with her father.

Meanwhile the newborn screening program started January 1, 1969. They tested for homocystinuria as well as PKU. In about two months they made their first diagnosis—homocystinuria, a rare hereditary disorder that is characterized by progressive physical and mental degeneration. Like PKU it is a disorder of amino acid metabolism so a person with homocystinuria is put on a special diet which is low in methionine. That particular person is probably still being monitored by Dr. David Pullon, the pediatrician involved in the diagnosis, who lives in Hamilton, an hour's drive south of Auckland.

In March of 1969 Bob began his travels to the islands of the South Pacific to make contact with those who were to be involved in the New Zealand screening program—which was his assignment according to the NIH grant that paid half of his salary for the year. First he flew to Honolulu where he bought a suit at Sears Roebuck before flying on to the end of the Trust Territories to the island of Saipan, the headquarters for the U.S. government's relationship with these territories. There are 2,200 islands in the Trust Territories with some 100,000 people. The Trust Territories, about 2,500 miles from side to side, are composed of several island groups—the Marshalls, the Mariannas and the Carolinas. On Saipan Bob spoke with the person in charge of the health system of these islands held in trust by the U.S. government. After meeting with an American doctor in Guam serving the American troops who were still stationed there, Bob began his tour. Continental Airlines flew through the Trust Territories only twice a week, so he found that he had to either stay in one location for three days or limit his visit to 45 minutes.

Bob was reminded of World War II wherever he went. At Truk there were numerous rusty war vehicles and tanks sitting around. The lagoon was littered with sunken Japanese ships. Met at the airport by the person who was to be involved in the screening program, Bob handed him some literature and gave him a short talk. That was it. In 45 minutes the plane was ready to leave and the meeting was over. In the Marshall Islands Bob stayed three days at Majuro Atoll. An atoll is a basin surrounded by a series of connected coral islands and Majuro Atoll in particular was a rude awakening for Bob. As usual he rose to the occasion. The town had a population of 4,000 and Bob stayed at a large old building serving as the hotel. He had his hair cut in what was called the "Biggest Barber Shop in the World." It was indeed big, but there was only one barber. The water was turned on for only an hour in the morning and an hour in the evening due to a chronic shortage. More rain catchment areas were in the planning stage, but not much work was being done on them and there were pigs and chickens wandering around the streets of town.

Bob became acquainted with two young men who were with the Peace Corps who had been working up north in a primitive area and were dazzled by the modern civilization of Majuro Atoll. The only high school in the Marshall Islands was on Majuro Atoll, so the students spent the school term there and then returned to their respective homes on a freighter that made the rounds of the islands. Bob was impressed by the children playing an energetic game of soccer, even though it was hot and muggy.

Bob met with ten or twelve medical people at Majuro Atoll, sharing information about PKU screening and testing for inborn errors of metabolism. He also learned something about medical innovations developed during World War II and met a man who had been a medical aide during the war, had been captured by the Japanese and placed in a prison camp where he continued in his medical role. He had been unable to get intravenous fluids, but found that coconut milk was sterile. So he had introduced the use of coconut milk for intravenous feedings and had published a paper on his innovation. After his escape from the prison camp during the war, he arrived in Majuro Atoll in a small boat with another escapee and had remained there ever since.

When the Continental airplane returned and it was time for Bob to leave, he found that the arrival of the plane was a special occasion. People came to watch it land and take off again. The concrete runway was nearly the length of the island and it was connected with a road at each end. In fact the runway was part of the road system for the island when the plane was not expected. The plane itself was a surprise. It looked very modern to Bob after Majuro Atoll, but it was a combination passenger-freight plane with the freight riding in the front behind a big netting in plain view of the passengers who sat in the back part of the cabin. But the flight attendants were pretty and wore big straw hats. Bob felt that he was on his way back to civilization.

Bob's next stop was Pago Pago in American Samoa where he made rounds with a doctor. He was told that American money was the ruination of Samoan family life: people had too much money. Traffic accidents were also a major problem. The doctor saw many children with ear infections; the largest part of his practice was prescribing antibiotics for them. In Pago Pago Bob tried to do some sailing. He and a medical aide rented a sunfish—a small sailboat—and paddled out to sea but since there was no wind, they merely drifted around. They had an adventure anyway for suddenly they found themselves directly in the path of a very long whale boat—the kind used 100 years ago on whaling ships—with some 50 men in the boat, each rowing for all he was worth. Bob's friend frantically tried to use the sailboat's centerboard to get out of the way. In the nick of time the coxswain on the whaling boat saw them and had everyone immediately cease rowing. All 50 turned around to see why they had stopped and laughed in a good-natured way. Bob learned that the islanders were fascinated with these long boats. Various towns in American Samoa had rowing contests each summer.

Western Samoa was next on Bob's agenda, a completely different experience from American Samoa for a tribal form of government governed their affairs. Each tribe had a chief and the chiefs met in a council. The people still lived in big thatched houses that were raised so they would get better air circulation. Family life was an improvement over that in American Samoa, but tuberculosis was a serious health problem. Bob met a World Health Organization medical officer who had come there to help advance the laboratory skills of local technicians.

The ethnic diversity of the people was intriguing to Bob. The doctor he contacted was a German who had gone to medical school in Germany. His wife was Polynesian. There were many similar families where the father was European, usually German, and the mother Polynesian. Apparently, at the time of World War I, Germany had taken over many of the islands in the South Pacific. During World War II Japan controlled many of them. It was an interesting interracial history to be explored. In Western Samoa Bob stayed at a hotel that was run by the woman who invented the Bloody Mary. It was also a place that was the basis for one of the stories in *Tales of the South Pacific* by James Michener. Before returning home Bob stopped in Nandi in the Fiji Islands and purchased a typewriter for his children, an umbrella and a little camera. When he arrived in the airport at Dunedin he was wearing the suit he had bought at Sears in Honolulu, carrying a hat for Jimmy from Majuro Atoll and toting the typewriter, umbrella and camera—obviously a well-traveled gentleman.

One of the things that had attracted Bob to New Zealand was the sailing. The farthest one can be from the ocean at any place in New Zealand is 80 miles and most places were much closer. So Bob now had time to indulge in his favorite sport. When he noticed an advertisement in the newspaper for a 16-foot boat called a Hartley trailer-sailor built of plywood, he couldn't resist. Mr. Hartley designed boats that were measured by the number of four-by-eight pieces of marine plywood used in the construction so they varied from twelve feet to 24 feet long. The owner of the advertised vessel (a doctor) had used it as a motorboat, but it could also be rigged as a sailboat. Bob and Margaret drove about 70 miles south of Dunedin in the red bus, bought the boat and towed it back to the Dunedin Motorboat and Yacht Club, the oldest yacht club in New Zealand. Bob used the length of chain he had carried on the trip across the U.S. in case one van had to be towed by the other in an emergency. Once the boat was in the water, the chain served to secure the anchor.

Bob hired a professional boat builder to hang the rudder on the back and make the center board trunk, but did the rest of the rigging himself on the weekends. He had the mast, boom, rigging wires and shroud sent down on a bus from Christchurch. Then he became aware of the nature of Christmastime in New Zealand. Since Christmas is at the height of the summer, many large shops and factories simply close down for two to three weeks and people go on vacation. Everyone worked feverishly to complete their business before they closed for Christmas, so Bob worked hard to get this boat ready before Christmas too.

In all, the family used the boat eleven times in New Zealand. They took a three-week camping trip during the Christmas holiday, driving around the south island with a dinghy on top of the red bus, pulling the boat on a trailer. They found the campgrounds in New

Zealand to be clean and inexpensive—costing about ten cents per person per day. The family made new friends all along the way and had several adventures. At one camp at Lake Wanecka in the center of the island Bob met another sailor, Dr. Noel Honey, whose son Neville later came to Buffalo to work at Roswell Park Institute on a fellowship in genetics before returning to New Zealand to teach genetics to undergraduate students at Palmerston North.

They stayed at one camp for five days, anchoring the boat on the water. Here Bob was impressed by the informality of check cashing in New Zealand. They had run out of cash and needed a few groceries. At the little market he was able to cash a check for $100 on his Dunedin account and purchase five dollars worth of supplies with no problem—a far cry from out-of-town check-cashing policies in much of the U.S. One night they camped by landing the boat at high tide on Adele Island, a place made famous during World War I. Count von Luckner, the German Sea Devil, had taken refuge there after escaping from prison in New Zealand, disrupting commerce by capturing many ships with what appeared to be an old sailing ship. In reality it was a modern battleship in disguise. He then kept the prisoners he captured in a large area below decks, setting them free on remote islands. The count maintained radio silence so it was difficult to locate him, although he was eventually recaptured. Johnny and Bob slept on the boat there and during the night heard a bumping noise. The next morning they found themselves high and dry several feet from the water—the bumping obviously caused by the movement of the boat when the tide went out.

Before leaving New Zealand Bob sold the boat for $600. He had spent a lot of money improving it so he took a loss, but the family's enjoyment had been worth it. The months in New Zealand passed quickly for the Guthries. They had made many friends and Bob had worked with a number of new colleagues. Johnny's sheltered workshop had also been a positive experience. Everyone in the family hated to leave, but all too soon it was time for them to trek on.

10

Around the World

In May 1969 when Bob Guthrie's sojourn at the University of Dunedin ended, it was time for the family to continue its journey around the world. They were to travel to Australia, South Africa, Spain, Italy, Switzerland, Germany, Norway, the other Scandinavian countries and the British Isles before boarding a ship for home. Such an adventure was not without its complications. They had planned to cross the Tasman Sea and tour Australia, but they learned that vehicles could not be sent on passenger ships, so they had to go by freighter. Bob sent the red bus by ship to Sydney a month ahead of time and then the family drove the camper to Christchurch where they could ship it to Melbourne. They planned to fly to Sydney, pick up their bus and then travel down the east coast to Melbourne where the green camper would be waiting for them.

Getting all seven Guthries and their luggage into one vehicle was no easy task and they were an arresting sight as they set off for Christchurch with two layers of luggage atop the van. On arriving in Melbourne they found Dr. David Pitt waiting for them—but not their green camper. A longshoreman's strike had left some 90 ships waiting out in the harbor, so there they stayed for ten days until their camper could be brought ashore. Dr. Pitt graciously arranged for them to stay in an unoccupied furnished staff house at the facility he directed. The delay allowed them to discover some interesting things about Australia. TV was different here than in Dunedin with its one black-and-white channel. Australia had several channels—all in color, but they also had commercials.

They were also intrigued by Australian politics. Since there are only six states, these tend to be much more powerful than in the U.S. To their surprise when they viewed a large railroad yard from a bridge, they found that the railroad tracks were not all the same distance apart. Those from New South Wales were a different gauge than those from Victoria—a vivid illustration of the independence of each state and the lack of agreement between them.

As was often the case, Bob mixed business with pleasure. In Adelaide he saw his family aboard an Italian ship, the *Marconi,* which was headed across the Indian Ocean to South Africa before he took off for two international meetings, one on screening in Tel Aviv, the other on phenylketonuria and related conditions in Heidelberg, Germany. Two weeks later on a flight to Durban, South Africa, to meet the *Marconi* he was quite pleased to be allowed to sit in the cockpit so he could get better pictures from the air. When he arrived in Durban, however, he learned his family's ship had been delayed for a day by a big storm at sea.

While he waited, Bob visited the department of pediatrics at the University of Natal—a university for "coloreds." Dr. Smythe, head of the department, admitted their budget was very low compared to that of the University of Johannesburg—which was for whites. Consequently newborn screening was a low priority since his main concern was the effect of undernutrition, especially protein depletion, on intelligence. He had just published a paper on this subject. Bob could understand his point of view and as a result of this encounter Bob wrote an article on this subject which was published on the front page of the NARC newsletter.

Finally the *Marconi* docked, so the family took a quick tour of the city and the beach area. They were much aware they were in a country where apartheid was the law of the land. Even in hard-hat areas they noticed that black workers tipped their hats when white workers passed.

Life aboard the *Marconi* was more informal than it had been on the British ship the family had taken to New Zealand. There were lots of parties and wine was always on the tables. Everyone enjoyed it, especially Anne and Barbara, as there were a thousand young Italian men on board completely outnumbering the women. As part of an agreement between Italy and Australia, these young men had spent two years working in Australia. Needless to say, Anne and Barbara did not lack for admirers and dancing partners. In fact, before the ship reached Italy, Anne and a young Italian man, Giovanni, had fallen in love. He was a nice young plumber by trade, but the shipboard romance disrupted the family's travel schedule.

Once the ship left South Africa, Bob hoped to resume his shipboard pastime of amateur navigation. After the junior officers discovered he was not trying to find the bathroom but only wanted to ask questions about navigation, they were attentive and helpful. When they were not on duty they would come looking for him and graciously answer his questions. To his great pleasure the ship's purser, impressed by Bob's credentials as a professor, took him up to the bridge and introduced him to the officers. The captain invited him to come up any time he wished, day or night. So Bob did. Jimmy and Patty no longer had to hide from him when it was time to shoot the sun. Up on the bridge Bob could get the position of the ship at any time by just comparing the navigator's position on the chart to his own.

There were short visits in the Canary Islands and Spain as the *Marconi* headed north toward the Mediterranean. Bob had hung an inflatable globe of the world in his cabin. One evening he noticed that if they maintained their speed of 600 miles a day, the next evening they should be near the Island of Stromboli with its active volcano. So the next evening Bob and Margaret went out on the deck at about ten p.m. It was dark but they looked in the direction where they thought Stromboli should be and suddenly the volcano erupted. Mother Nature's fireworks were most appropriate as it was the third of July.

Arriving in Naples, they bid the *Marconi* adieu, took the vans off the ship and broke out their camping gear. This was to be the starting point for their European adventure. However, the romance between Anne and Giovanni had not cooled. So the Guthries along with Giovanni, instead of going north as planned, headed south to meet his family. By this time they had camping down to a science. They would park the two buses parallel to each other with the sliding doors opposite each other so a canvas awning could be stretched between the two vehicles. A ridge pole in the center held up a fluorescent light that operated off of the cigarette lighter in one of the buses. That was the kitchen area. Each person had a specific job to do so they could set up camp in a hurry. Johnny looked for water. Jimmy set up the stove and got it going. Barbara and Anne pulled out the sleeping bags and duffel bags.

Giovanni's family lived in the little town of Montescolioso at the southernmost tip of the Italian boot. Their progress was slowed by numerous flat tires. Bob ultimately discovered the reason was that while the buses had been on board ship, the wheels had not been blocked. Consequently every time the ship rolled, the wheels were knocked out of alignment.

Giovanni's father was an important person in Montescolioso, probably the second most important after the priest for he was in charge of the water supply. The Guthries descended upon the family and everyone was quite friendly, in spite of the language barrier. They could speak no English, the Guthries could speak no Italian. Their house was built around a large water tank with each room on a higher level than the previous one. The top of the tank was higher than all the other structures in the town—except the steeple of the church. The town was old and picturesque, horse-drawn wagons traveled the streets. The Guthries spent the evening with Giovanni's family and after dinner they all sat around smiling at each other, watching Italian TV. When the Guthries left Montescolioso, they were accompanied by Giovanni's mother and sister, who had decided to travel with them as far as Rome, riding in the red bus with Anne and Barbara.

Before leaving Montescolioso Bob had taken Anne and Giovanni aside and made an agreement with them. If 60 days after Anne got back to the United States, she and Giovanni still wanted to get married, Bob would guarantee Giovanni financially so he could emigrate to the U.S. Bob said it was one of the smartest things he ever did in his life. It turned out that well before the 60 days at home had passed Anne realized it would be a mistake to marry Giovanni, a man she hardly knew. She turned to the International Institute at the University of Buffalo for help in writing a gentle letter in Italian suggesting they should reconsider their plan to marry.

After this the family had a whirlwind tour of Italy, missing some of the cities they had intended to visit such as Genoa and Venice, as the trip to Montescolioso had taken two weeks of the six weeks they had set aside to spend in Europe. They had arranged hard-to-get reservations for their two vehicles on ferry boats from Norway to England and from England to Ireland so they could not afford to linger. Anne and Barbara thoroughly enjoyed the drive through Europe. There was plenty of room in their camper and there were lots of good-looking young men hitchhiking. So they made frequent stops. It was always disconcerting to them and their guests to hear Bob's voice over the CB inquiring about the delay. He felt it was good insurance to let the hitchhikers know there was someone in the bus ahead who was responsible for the two girls who had picked them up.

The Guthries had planned to go north from Italy through a tunnel to Switzerland, but as they climbed ever higher, one of the hitchhikers in the girls' vehicle pointed out that Bob had missed the road to the tunnel. So they all continued right over the top of the Alps. They camped for five days near Heidelberg while Bob spent time with Professor Horst Bickel, the first person to develop a low-phenyl-alanine formula.

While they were there the U.S. astronauts were scheduled to land on the moon, so the family rose early the morning of the landing and Bob plugged the TV into the cigarette lighter. They arranged themselves to watch the spectacle only to discover that the landing had taken place the night before. It had been scheduled to occur during prime time for American audiences, so they went to Dr. Bickel's house to watch a rerun on his color TV set.

Driving on the autobahns in Germany proved to be a challenge to the Guthries and somewhat distressing to the German motorists. The two buses could travel a little faster than the trucks in the right lane, but they couldn't move fast enough to suit the people speeding along in regular passenger cars. Bob instructed Barbara to stay right behind him so that they wouldn't get separated in the line of trucks. When he was ready to pass, he would let her know and the two vehicles would pull into the fast lane and slowly pass the trucks. Quite a long line of cars would collect behind them before they could return to the slow lane in front of the trucks. Some of the frustrated drivers displayed their displeasure by blinking their lights and shaking their fists at them as they drove by.

A hasty tour of the Scandinavian countries allowed Bob to visit the John Kennedy Center in Copenhagen where, as early as 1962, they had been using Bob's test. In fact, Erna Lund had been testing 10,000 to 12,000 babies a year for PKU, histidinemia, methionine and galactosemia. The rocky terrain covered with evergreen trees in Sweden reminded Bob very much of Minnesota and he understood why many Norwegians and Swedes had settled that state. The son of Asbjörn Fölling, the doctor who first described PKU, escorted the family into Oslo, Norway, and had them stay in his parents' flat, since his father and mother were at their summer home. In Dr. Fölling's flat Bob saw his Kennedy Award, a beautiful winged angel in Steubenware, sitting on a shelf. The next night was spent at the summer home of the Föllings.

Traveling south, they were overawed by the beautiful fjords they passed as they headed for the large ferry that would take them to Newcastle-on-Tyne in England. Touring the British Isles was a distinct pleasure. With the exception of Wales, they were back to English-speaking countries. In Edinburgh they were treated like visiting royalty by Jim Farquhar, one of the pioneers in screening for PKU in Scotland. Traveling inland the family hunted for the Guthrie Castle, a treat Bob had been anticipating for a long time. They found Guthrie to be just a wide place in the road with the castle and the Guthrie church ready to be explored. Their unofficial tour guide was the same person who ran the post office. Church records revealed a long list of ministers and some of them had been Guthries. They were told that the castle would not remain in the Guthrie line because it was always inherited by a male heir. The present male heir, John Guthrie, was mentally retarded. This statement was made to Bob while Johnnie was standing nearby. Fortunately he was not paying attention.

The castle was a private residence so they were not allowed inside, but they spent most of the day on the grounds enjoying their beauty and peace. Built as a summer home and not for military purposes, there was only one tower with parapets for defense. That night the family camped by a little nearby lake. Another night was spent at Loch Lomond allowing them to admire Ben Lomond through their binoculars. Arriving in Belfast, Ireland, they drove south to Dublin where they set up camp in the backyard of Dr. Seamus Cahalane—who had eight children, ensuring that the Guthrie children would have a great time. Bob and Seamus had become fast friends ever since Seamus had almost single-handedly organized screening in the Republic of Ireland making it one of the first countries in the world to have nationwide screening. As it turned out, the incidence of PKU in Ireland is about one in 5,000 births, more than twice the rate in the United States. Dr. Cahalane also diagnosed a number of cases of galactosemia, homocystinuria and maple syrup urine disease, all disorders detected by tests developed in Bob's lab.

Finally it was back to England to board their ship home. As they drove through the Welsh countryside the Guthries noticed that the English sheep all had tails. Their awareness of sheep had heightened while living in New Zealand where all the sheep had their tails cut off. They continued on and camped at a place called Glass Palace that was quite convenient for sightseeing in London. The underground took them from camp right into the city. They also renewed acquaintance with two brothers they had met in Italy who invited them to visit their house in London. The brothers saw them off, riding behind them on motorcycles to Southhampton where the family boarded a Holland-American line ship bound for the U.S.A.

The ship was more luxurious than any they had yet sailed on—and it was more expensive. But Bob felt it was worth the added cost. They had three staterooms with portholes that were actually above the water line. What Bob did not realize was that their cabins were right above the ship's screws which created so much vibration at night it felt like they were sleeping in the flatbed of a truck. Once they got used to it, all was well. Besides, no one stayed inside much in the daytime anyway. As they left Southhampton they saw the sleek *Queen Elizabeth II* speed by them on its way to England. Before they reached New York City she passed them again headed for America.

Bob had planned to do more navigation on the return trip, but he was prevented by cloudy weather, so he played a lot of chess, practicing on Jimmy and later joining a tournament with a fellow faculty member from the University of Buffalo. To Bob's surprise he won the tournament in spite of the fact that he had not played for a long time. His opponent was rather disgruntled.

The ship arrived in New York Harbor early one morning and the family turned out on deck to see the Statue of Liberty. They went under the bridge that goes to Staten Island so Bob took a picture of Barbara looking at the hospital where she was born. After docking and disembarking on the shores of the Hudson River, they watched as their cars were hoisted out of the ship. Later they toured New York City on foot—like foreign tourists—taking pictures from the top of the Empire State Building of their ship heading back out to sea.

The reality of being back in the U.S.A. dawned on them when Bob had great difficulty cashing a check at a branch of a bank where he had an account. It would have been easier in New Zealand, but it was nice to be home anyway. The family drove north, camping along the way at the homes of friends, arriving back in Williamsville in time for the children to return to school in September.

When the Guthrie children told their friends they had traveled around the world in two VW buses, they were greeted with expressions of disbelief. It was a great adventure. Bob and Margaret never regretted all the work and planning that had been necessary to make their family adventure a success.

The Guthries camping with their two V.W. buses

The faithful V.W. boarding ship in England for the last leg of their round-the-world journey

11

John Guthrie Grows Up

"Well, I guess this is the last supper," said Bob as he gazed proudly around the dinner table at his assembled family. They were all home at the same time and it probably would not happen again for a long time. But Johnny interrupted the sentimental moment asking, "The last supper? Who's getting crucified?" Such was his droll sense of humor.

As he grew older Johnny developed a more definitive personality. His speech was never clear so most people had difficulty understanding him. Johnny realized this and was very sensitive about it. Asked his name, he would walk away rather than undergo the embarrassment of answering. He became a shy person and a loner, however with people who understood him he displayed a large vocabulary and a great sense of humor.

John had a highly developed sense of right and wrong. On one occasion some friends with a new baby visited Bob and Margaret. The baby was asleep when they arrived and not wanting to disturb it they left it sleeping in the car. A few minutes later Johnny came storming into the house wanting to know why those "hippies" had left a baby alone in the car.

He rarely used proper names, making up nicknames for everyone. His brother Jim was "The Kid." Patty was "Hot Pants" when she was a teenager. He called his brother Tom "Poison Man." Bob was "Gorilla" or "Horspistal" or "The Guy With Glasses." Hester the cat was "The Meow." His brother-in-law Richard was "That Hippie" and Margaret was "The Lady." Johnny also had definite likes and dislikes about clothing, preferring sweatshirts and jeans to anything else. He called dress shirts and slacks "tuxedos" and owned only one nice suit for special occasions.

Food was important to him. He did not like meat with bones, but preferred hamburger. Ice cubes were high on his list so he made sure the trays were filled. He always needed to know what he would be having for the next meal. Food he didn't like was called "foreign food." He slept with earplugs to cut out noise and never opened his window at night, winter or summer. He kept an electric fan going in the summer. In winter he sometimes had a heater and a fan running simultaneously. As an adult he continued to keep his stuffed animals on his bed and sometimes he carried them around the house. A huge stuffed banana highlighted the collection. Several sun dresses could be found laid out on his bed as well, perhaps as substitutes for girlfriends.

Fascinated with black people, Johnny got excited when he saw them. At one point he had a black girlfriend named Versie and sometimes Bob and Margaret would take the two of them to lunch. Johnny wanted to marry her but she eventually moved on to another boyfriend. After his disappointment he got a black doll he named Versie. John also held definite opinions about spare-time activities. He never went to movies, calling them "horror films." His TV watching consisted of the news, weather reports and cartoons. Home slide shows were a different matter however. He would often ask his dad for a slide show whenever he was home—with the condition that the six-foot banana could watch too. Some magazines held John's attention, especially the *National Geographic,* and he enjoyed having articles read to him from the newspaper.

Natural disasters like earthquakes, tornadoes and volcanos were intriguing to Johnny. He paid close attention to the weather forecast and could always tell you when inclement weather was coming. If a toilet overflowed or if a fire engine or ambulance went by, he was delighted. According to his brother-in-law Richard Gaeta with whom he had a good relationship, he was a "disaster freak." Model trains were a great love of Johnny's and Bob indulged him in this. He had a train table in the basement and Johnny was a member of a historical train society. Margaret would accompany him to meetings. She also took him on occasional excursions sponsored by the various train societies on old trains that run 20 or 30 miles through the country. They would attend train shows where he could purchase used engines and parts which he carefully inspected before buying. His parents believed that his main interest in trains was getting them repaired. They were constantly getting broken and the people at the repair shop were well acquainted with their regular customer John Guthrie.

After the family returned from New Zealand Johnny continued to live at home. He attended Niagara Frontier Vocational Center where he had several weeks of evaluation and did some assembly work and food service. He learned to travel to the center by public transportation. At first Bob was so concerned that John might get confused that he followed the bus in his car several days in a row. He was relieved and pleased when he saw that Johnny always got off at the right stop.

His brothers and sisters had mixed feelings about John. As children they felt protective of him. Even so, they had to admit that they were also a little embarrassed by him and didn't want to go out in public with him. They defended him when they saw other children tease him, yet they sometimes teased him themselves. They knew he received a great deal of special attention from their parents. Anne, two years younger than John, became his first playmate and she probably understood him better than any of the others. As he grew older, John developed a temper and was easily frustrated. When angered he would throw his glasses or his lunch pail on the ground. Occasionally he would lash out at Margaret, his constant companion, kicking or hitting her. Of course this was difficult for Margaret but it was especially upsetting to the other children.

As his brothers and sisters grew up and went away to school and to work, Johnny became increasingly lonely. Tom and Barbara were in Seattle; Jim and Patty no longer lived at home. Anne had met Richard and they were working in a group home in Buffalo. Realizing that one day they would have to find another home for John, Anne urged her parents to look into the possibility of a group home for him. It seemed likely John would outlive Bob and Margaret and it was important for him to be used to living apart from them when that eventuality arrived.

In the late 1970s John began interviews for applications to group homes, but he made it perfectly clear he did not want to move. He also had some speech lessons with a therapist who took him to various stores and restaurants where he was to communicate with waitresses and clerks. He made every effort to improve his speaking skills, but did not make much lasting progress. A home trainer taught him such skills as bed-making, simple cooking and shopping.

In 1980 when John was 33, Bob was to return to New Zealand for a six-month sabbatical leave and Margaret was to accompany him. This was the impetus for actually moving Johnny to the group home. It was difficult for him, but it was even more difficult for Margaret. Bob felt that Margaret needed Johnny as much as he needed her. The group home they chose was less than a mile from their house in Williamsville, allowing her to see him often when she was in town. After visiting the facility Johnny agreed to "try it out." But he did everything he could to make Bob and Margaret feel guilty. He called it "the institution" and the people who lived there "inmates." On his first night as a resident he ran away and came home. One of the staff people promptly arrived and took him back to the facility. He ran home once or twice after that, but finally accepted his new living arrangement.

While Bob and Margaret were in New Zealand—from September 1980 to March, 1981—John did very well. Anne, Richard and

Jim were staying at the house on Academy Street, so Johnny had a place to visit on weekends. One of the prerequisites for living at the group home was that Johnny had to have an outside activity five days a week. This was no problem since he had been working at the Northtown's Branch of Allentown Industry for ten years. The workshop was located less than a mile away from his home and it operated a highly successful furniture refinishing business. Johnny walked to work unless he could convince Margaret to drive him. He sometimes complained about the "bossy" girls, although he had a girlfriend who also worked there. He refused to carry his lunch and would use part of his salary to buy one daily.

Although Johnny tried various positions, he seemed most content in one of the lowest paying, least skilled jobs, rubbing tung oil on furniture all day. The workshop director felt he was capable of doing more advanced work, such as stripping, for which he would have earned a larger salary, but Johnny was not successful in any other category of work. Bob felt that although his son was capable of more complicated work, Johnny did not want the added responsibility of a more technical job. He preferred the ease of applying the tung oil. Johnny earned about ten percent of the minimum wage—enough to pay for his lunches—because he accomplished only about ten percent of the average productivity. A monthly SSI check came from the state, indirectly from the federal government. Most of this was used to pay for the group home, but a small portion was for spending money—spent mostly on diet cokes, but he did save enough for an annual holiday trip supervised by the group home staff.

Bob was not satisfied with the workshop for he had seen workshops in other countries that focused more on discovering the needs of the individual clients and then developing programs to fit those needs. Ultimately Johnny adjusted well to the group home. He was well liked by the staff and the other interesting residents. There were ten adults, including four women. His first roommate had been a friend since they were in Boy Scouts together and there was an outgoing woman in the home in her 60s with rugged features named

Theresa plus two residents with Down syndrome. Johnny became very much a part of the scene.

Over the years Johnny changed rooms and roommates several times and there were also turnovers in the staff at the group home. He adjusted to these changes without much difficulty. He was well-behaved and compliant, never needing much supervision. He got up early, made his bed and put his clothes away (which he did not do at home), and he did his share of the chores. He had trouble combing his hair and shaving, but he improved over time. He was attentive to his teeth and did a lot of flossing. His dentist received the nickname "mouth-bleeder." His worst complaint was usually about television sets. Most of the residents had them in their rooms and some had stereos and VCRs. Johnny liked to watch TV by himself as he didn't approve of most programs the others watched. The only time problems arose was when he became frustrated or when he did not want to obey the staff. Then he kicked people.

Johnny kept his collection of stuffed "friends" in his room at the group home and often played with them. Whenever he felt uncomfortable in a conversation he "talked" through them. If someone asked an embarrassing question he would respond with, "Banana Man says this" or "Celery Man says that." Sometimes John walked around his neighborhood just to see what was going on. When he was alone in his room he had long conversations with unseen persons, creations of his vivid imagination. Mainly Johnny continued the habit he had established early—watching other people.

There were many leisure activities in which Johnny seldom participated. Bob had set up a train table for him in the basement of the group home and Johnny preferred playing there to going to the movies (he said they were too bloody) or watching TV. He was rough with his trains. Bob tried to explain to him that this was the reason they were constantly getting broken, but to no avail. Johnny always seemed delighted to have to go to the repair shop. On one of his birthdays, Bob bought him a big train, an LGB, which is larger than the Lionel. He later added another engine and a couple of coaches for it, but they did not satisfy John because they were so sturdy they never got broken. When he was given to outbursts of temper he threw things. On some occasions, anticipating an outburst over some difference with the staff, he would take his trains home the previous day so that he would not cause irreparable damage to them.

In later years Johnny developed mild diabetes, gout and elevated blood pressure. He was on oral medication for the diabetes and he was faithful to his diet. He loved diet Pepsi—but did not like going to gatherings where cookies, cake or other goodies he could not eat were served. Johnny enjoyed excursions in the sailboat with Bob, usually staying down in the cabin. But if the wind died down and Bob had to start the auxiliary motor, he was most pleased. He would stick his head up through the companionway and say with a smile, "White things on strike!" On one occasion Bob sailed his boat north from Florida. John and Margaret joined him in Troy and came through the Erie Canal with him on the boat. Johnny especially enjoyed helping at the locks. On another occasion Bob could not get the engine started and Johnny suggested he check the fuel line. Bob demurred and got a mechanic who found that there was indeed something wrong with the fuel line.

Traveling and camping continued to be great favorites of Johnny's. His parents took him as far away as Vancouver to visit Tom and his family. He called Tom's children "The Infants" even after they became teenagers. In addition to family travels, he went on a supervised trip nearly every year. The group home's eight or ten residents would be accompanied by two staff members in a van from New York state. They stayed in motels and had an excursion each day going to places like Maine, Cape Cod and Baltimore. Johnny's favorite trip was a ride on the *Delta Queen*, up the Mississippi River from New Orleans. He saved his money for these trips and kept hoping one day for a Caribbean cruise or a vacation in Hawaii.

The director of his group home believed Johnny was more capable than his parents gave him credit for and thought his parents had sheltered him too much. Bob and Margaret agreed this was probably true. They had two telephones and Johnny knew both numbers. For years he would call Margaret every morning at seven and again every afternoon when he got home from work, reporting the events of his day. In some ways Johnny was Margaret's confidant as well; they would listen as each told the other about the details of their lives. According to the director of the group home, John chose to communicate with and through his parents rather than directly with the staff and his peers. He would not initiate conversations, but would listen and then tell his parents about what had gone on. A number of times he convinced his parents to mediate for him with the staff. He obviously needed help communicating with people.

Although his workshop was only about a mile from the group home, he usually tried to get Margaret to drive him to work. If the weather was inclement, he would point out that it was cloudy, threatening rain and thunder. During the winter he complained that the sidewalks were too snowy and the cars did not stop, nearly hitting him when he crossed Main Street. Much of the time Margaret complied and drove him to work, picking him up again in the afternoon, especially in the winter. When the workshop moved further away, John began to ride to work on a regular basis with others from his group home. In addition to daily telephone calls home and getting rides to work from Margaret, John came home every other weekend. Margaret would take him out to lunch, usually at McDonald's. They sometimes went bowling and she and Johnny would go grocery shopping. John still had a bedroom at home so in essence he had two homes.

The philosophy of the group home was that the clients should develop independence. Members of the staff worried about what would happen to John when his parents were no longer alive. They were sure he had some reading ability because as a client he helped with the grocery shopping and he had demonstrated that he could shop from a grocery list. A volunteer worked with Johnny from time to time to improve his reading skills. John also attended "night school" at Buffalo State College with his group, learning about independent living.

In 1992 John was in counseling with a psychotherapist at Catholic Charities and Bob and Margaret attended some of the sessions. One issue was that John became especially fearful on the rare occasions when his parents were both out of town at the same time. He worried about what "country" they had gone to. Margaret and Bob explored their feelings and their relationship with John finding ways to help him express himself better, empowering him to have more control over his life.

The staff members felt that John could have moved on in the system of the facility. This would have involved living in a "supportive apartment" situation where the client does his own shopping, prepares his own meals and goes to work independently. John budgeted his money on a two-weeks basis and knew his proper diet. He kept a 30-day supply of his medication in his lock box and administered this himself. In addition he walked to the bank to deposit his check and to the drug store to pick up his medication. Bob and Margaret wanted him to develop more independence but they would have been deeply concerned if he had moved into a "supportive apartment" at that time. Richard, John's brother-in-law and one of John's best friends, agreed that John was much smarter than anyone realized. He believed that much of what came out of the Guthrie house came out of the mouth of Johnny. He also felt that John had a great deal of control over his parents.

John undoubtedly influenced the career decisions of several members of his family. Anne got a master's degree and has made a career of working with the families of adults with mental handicaps in New York City. Richard, her husband, is a playwright whose plays are about people with mental retardation. Patty, a newspaper reporter in Albuquerque, New Mexico, has taken a special interest in writing about Native Americans with fetal alcohol syndrome. Her review of the book *The Broken Cord*, the story of a child suffering from fetal alcohol syndrome, was published in the *New York Times* July 30,

1989. She was recently selected as one of 13 American journalists to be awarded Nieman fellowships to study at Harvard University where she will focus on Native Americans and public health.

While moving Johnny to the group home left a void in Margaret's life after devoting so many years to his constant care, she soon realized that this arrangement was much better for him. This also freed her to do volunteer work. She delivered food for Meals On Wheels and worked at a thrift shop. The Red Cross, the Adult Advisement Center at the University, ARC and church groups all benefited from her involvement.

Despite the busy lives that Bob and Margaret lead, it was obvious that Johnny was a high priority with them. Of the six Guthrie children, only Johnny continued to live near his parents. As Margaret put it, he added an "interesting dimension" to their lives. Through him they learned patience and gained a deeper understanding of persons with disabilities.

12

New Frontiers

It was the fall of 1962 and an expectant crowd had gathered in the school auditorium to learn which community resident would be recognized for his or her outstanding service and contribution to public education. No one knew who had been selected, as the speaker was enumerating and extolling the accomplishments of the honoree. He had been a supporter of the local public schools since arriving in Williamsville in 1954 and his six children had all attended public schools.

The honoree had attended school board meetings and, most importantly, taken an active part in getting school bond issues passed at election time. The school population had outgrown most of the facilities in the community and many classes were being held in temporary or relocatable rooms that received no support from the state. If the bond issues could be passed, permanent rooms could be added to the schools and these would receive 50 percent state aid, but the voters needed to be convinced. They had to be shown that, over a period of years, they would actually save money. This determined man, a traveling salesman at heart, had joined the planning sessions of the committee working to pass the bond issues, attending meetings twice and sometimes three times a week. Supporters of the bond issues were identified and precinct captains were assigned to secure their votes. The person being honored had convinced 400 people to deliver ten votes apiece. That equaled 4,000 votes—enough for passage. For the first time in many years a bond issue was approved two-to-one and permanent additions were to replace the temporary classrooms at the six elementary schools in the community.

In the early '60s this person had garnered National Science Foundation support for a summer science program for high-achieving high school students. The first summer only 30 students could be accepted out of 500 applicants. They came from all over the country and spent eight weeks at the new Mill Middle School where the program was held. This man had been head of the committee that had planned the excellent science laboratories and directed the program. For every five students there was a high school science teacher and for every two high school teachers there was a university faculty member. Each week a lecture was given by a visiting scientist. Otherwise, there were no regular classes. The students had a choice of chemistry, physics or biology.

The program grew each summer to a maximum of 60 students and it moved to the university. The National Science Foundation staff who came for a site visit were impressed with the program and the director was equally impressed with the young people who participated. He found them to be bright and attractive young people, ethnically and culturally mixed. They had a tremendous interest in each other's points of view and were reading books about serious subjects—politics, sex, the war in Vietnam—books the director never would have read at that age. Later he learned that in the evenings when they were supposed to be sleeping, the students often held "rap sessions," talking about every subject under the sun. After directing the program for three summers, thoroughly enjoying it, the director found he just could not keep up the exhausting schedule any longer.

This person had a particular interest in children with mental disabilities, as well as those who were gifted. Since children were being bused to school, he thought a plan might be devised in which children who were gifted could be bused along with children with disabilities. It had been his experience that children who are gifted get along very well with others. He believed the two groups of children would stimulate each other and it would be beneficial for both. This idea was discussed with the superintendent of the Buffalo schools and some of his own colleagues; however nothing came of it because of the difficult logistics.

Interestingly enough, in 1960 Supreme Court Justice William O. Douglas had addressed a meeting in Williamsville. Following the meeting there had been a discussion asking Mr. Douglas whether he felt it would be appropriate for children with mental retardation to attend public schools along with children without disabilities. Justice Douglas thought for a few moments and then replied that it certainly seemed like a good idea; furthermore, if a suit on the question was ever filed and reached the Supreme Court, he would vote in favor of the idea.

The idea of "mainstreaming" children with disabilities into the regular schools came into vogue some years later as professionals became increasingly aware that isolating groups of children from others was wrong. Children without disabilities can learn tolerance and understanding by associating with those with mental retardation while children with mental disabilities can certainly learn many things from children without disabilities. The honoree had become particularly interested in some individual students who were gifted and who had come to him for advice about their future plans. He had given several of them summer jobs in his lab and was pleased to feel that he had a part in shaping their careers. Not everything in the schools was to his liking, however, and he had made his views known. He was not always able to effect the changes he wanted, but it was not for lack of trying.

In addition to working with high school students, this person had participated in the science fair for elementary school children in Williamsville. For the benefit of second and fourth graders, he developed a science program in which he and two assistants did demonstrations with microscopic animals called hydra. He brought along

20 low-power microscopes so the children could watch brine shrimp larvae, which appeared to be little dots when viewed with the naked eye, being grabbed by the tentacles of the hydra. There had been many questions and much discussion by the children, and the program had been a huge success.

This man had also arranged a Saturday class at the Buffalo Science Museum for one year. The children from Williamsville were transported there by bus. In addition, each year he had found time to visit the special education class in the local school and talk to the children about what it is like to be a scientist. The person being honored was also well-known professionally. In 1961 this prestigious citizen had developed a special test for a disorder that, untreated, caused mental retardation. There had been articles about him, not only in professional journals, but in newspapers and magazines across the country. His picture had even been in *Life* magazine.

By the end of the speech everyone knew that the honor was going to Dr. Robert Guthrie and that it was well deserved. As he waited in the wings to walk on stage and receive the award, Bob saw an American history book on the piano, and noted that the preface talked about "America, the Melting Pot." As the speaker continued telling about the achievements of this outstanding citizen, Bob thought about the suburb of Williamsville with its upper-middle-class population. He knew what he would see when he walked out onto the stage—a sea of white faces. Not one Afro-American person would be in the audience. Williamsville was not a melting pot, Bob realized. It was a "white ghetto." For some time he had been involved in race relations and had started a discussion group on equal housing opportunities at his local Presbyterian church, but the interest had not been overwhelming. A group of 20 some people met for a year at the church and Bob had shown the group a film on genetics, demonstrating there was no genetic difference between races, but the elders of the church decided they should not be sponsoring this "trouble-making" group so they were renamed the Church and Society Committee which would deal, first, with separation of church and state. This effectively ended Bob's discussion group.

The minister of the church, however, became involved in politics and ran for a position on the school board in 1970. He favored an interdistrict plan for the voluntary busing of a hundred Afro-American kindergarten children into the local schools. The issue was emotionally charged and the whole campaign had focused on it. By the time the minister lost the race, Bob had learned how racist the community was.

Recalling all this, Bob's acceptance speech evaporated from his mind when the applause died down, and he took the podium. Looking out over the assembled citizens of Williamsville, he spoke from his heart and told them they could not really educate children in their community unless other people were allowed to live there. And he used the term "white ghetto" in describing Williamsville.

Although there was not one African-American person in the audience, there was a reporter there from the Buffalo Evening News. The story which appeared the next day along with a picture of Bob bannered the headline, "Guthrie Claims Williamsville is a White Ghetto." Shortly, Bob began receiving hate mail and crank phone calls. People even sent him his picture clipped from the paper with "Communist Agent" written under it. His children remember being somewhat embarrassed at the time, but they all agree now that their father was on the right side of social issues.

Regardless of the repercussions from his speech, Bob was extremely proud of the award he received that night. Again, in the fall of 1970, Bob received further recognition. A school was dedicated to him. He was the only person chosen for this honor who was not a school board member or employee. A bronze plaque is permanently installed in the Mill Middle School, bearing the words: "This school is dedicated to Robert Guthrie whose high expectations and constant endeavor to attain excellence in education provided an unyielding challenge for its accomplishment in the Williamsville school district."

Throughout the years, organizations of parents and friends of people with mental disabilities have been instrumental in bringing about many positive changes. These organizations first concentrated on changing the attitude of the public toward people with retardation—from an attitude of fear and rejection to one of acceptance and understanding. They worked to change the practice of confining people with mental disability in large, prison-like institutions where, in earlier years, they had been warehoused along with people suffering from mental illness. Parents were often the ones who refused to listen to the doctors who tended to advise immediate institutionalization for an infant with mental retardation.

The National Association for Retarded Children (now the Association for Retarded Citizens) was established in 1950. But as late as 1953 a well-known medical textbook said of persons with mental retardation that "Institutional training is the best available form of treatment." Although researchers were expanding the body of knowledge regarding the causes of various types of mental retardation, parents' groups often primarily concentrated on the welfare and training of those who were already mentally disabled. They held the philosophy that, as much as possible, people with mental disabilities should lead normal lives.

The idea of sending children with mental retardation to regular schools came into vogue, even if it meant a child had to be in special education classes. This allowed children with mental handicaps to socialize with other children, joining scout troops and bowling leagues, bicycling and taking excursions, and competing in the Special Olympics. Sheltered workshops were established, allowing adults with handicaps to perform meaningful work and earn small salaries.

One example of parent-power is RETAP, a local organization devoted to helping adults with mental retardation in Erie County, New York. Bob Guthrie and two of his friends started that organization more than 25 years ago. From the beginning Margaret and Bob were active volunteers and board members. RETAP runs a thrift shop which raises cash to be used for grants to persons or other organizations that provide services to adults with mental disabilities. Bob and Margaret became convinced that a huge potential existed for the use of computers with adults who are mentally retarded. Computers could be put in group homes and used by the residents for fun and games, as well as for academic achievement. RETAP is currently raising funds to support graduate studies at New York State University at Buffalo for those working for advanced degrees in this area. No doubt many such local organizations exist across the country, providing needed services to this population.

As knowledge about the causes of various forms of mental retardation has grown in the medical community and new scientific advances have been achieved, the concept of prevention has steadily come to the fore. By the 1960s doctors began talking about "inborn errors of metabolism," a term coined by Archibald Garrod in 1908. He had published a paper in 1902 entitled "The Incidence of Alkaptonuria, A Study in Chemical Individuality" which, a half-century ahead of its time, showed insight into the inheritance of specific chemical defects in metabolism and demonstrated that an enzyme deficiency can be inherited and lead to disease. Archibald Garrod was later knighted, becoming Sir Archibald Garrod.

By the 1970s doctors began telling parents' groups that with the tools then available to the medical profession, it was possible to cut the rate of mental retardation in half. Prevention became one of the most exciting aspects in the field of mental retardation. Bob Guthrie's development of the technique of using a dried-blood spot on filter paper for newborn screening opened unlimited possibilities in prevention. After he and his staff added galactosemia and maple syrup urine disease as well as PKU to the list of disorders that could be identified by the bacterial inhibition assay technique, he continued to broaden his research. Between 1964 and 1967 tests for two more hereditary disorders were developed in his lab: homocystinuria and tyrosinemia. Like PKU, homocystinuria causes mental retardation and can be treated by diet.

Between 1970 and 1972 Dr. Michael Garrick, working in Bob Guthrie's lab, developed another important test that can be done on the blood specimen taken for PKU. This test is for sickle cell disease, a serious hereditary disorder in which some red blood cells are shaped like crescents or sickles. They interfere with the normal transport of oxygen and can cause severe anemia and bone pain. Early death is commonly caused by secondary bacterial infection. Dr. Garrick's studies were reported in the *New England Journal of Medicine* in 1993. Screening has now become a standard of practice throughout the United States even though this disorder can also be diagnosed prenatally. (Sickle cell disease is discussed in greater detail in the appendix of this book.)

Dr. Jean Dussault of Quebec made an important contribution to the prevention of mental retardation in the 1970s by developing a test for congenital hypothyroidism, a disorder that has been estimated to be as frequent as one in 3,500 births worldwide. This test is now being used in most of the places where the PKU test is done. If undiagnosed and untreated, patients with hypothyroidism are short and pudgy with coarse facial features, sparse hair, dry skin and mental retardation. Approximately 95 percent of these cases are not hereditary and the treatment is quite simple and inexpensive once diagnosis is made. The patient is given thyroid hormone orally and mental retardation is prevented.

Biotinidase deficiency is a disorder in which a baby lacks the enzyme needed for recycling biotin—one of the B vitamins. This results in severe clinical symptoms, including developmental delay and mental retardation. It is easily treated by adding extra biotin to the diet. Dr. Barry Wolf developed the test for this disorder and it is now available. Tests have also been developed for congenital adrenal hyperplasia and for congenital toxoplasmosis. The latter test is used on all PKU specimens collected in the state of Oregon. Cystic fibrosis is another serious disorder that can be diagnosed from the dried-blood spot. While it does not cause mental retardation, the symptoms are severe and screening is presently being done in

Australia, New Zealand and the states of Colorado and Wisconsin. Bob's hope was that every state would test for this disorder.

To help authorities monitor the spread of AIDS, the dried-blood-spot technique can also be used to test for the HIV antibody. In nearly every state of the United States, the specimen taken for PKU screening is now also screened for HIV antibody activity. Adenosine deaminase (ADA) deficiency is a rare disorder that prevents the immune system of the body from fighting off viral and bacterial infections. Only some 25 children are born with this disorder in the U.S. each year. Infants with ADA deficiency nearly always die during childhood from infections. One well-publicized case in Houston involved a child who had immunodeficiency disease who became known as the "bubble boy" because he was shielded from all sources of infection. He died at the age of twelve in 1984.

In an exciting new development Dr. Donald B. Kohn and a team of researchers at Childrens Hospital of Los Angeles announced in May, 1995 that they had successfully performed gene therapy on two children with ADA deficiency, isolating white blood cells from the infants' umbilical cords at birth, altering the cells so they began to produce ADA and reinfused the cells into the infants four days later. The children who were treated at birth are now two years old and it appears that their cures will be permanent. While the technique is not yet perfected, it holds the promise of treatment for a broad variety of genetic diseases. ADA deficiency can be diagnosed with the dried-blood-spot technique and the state of New York presently screens for this disorder.

So while the PKU test was the first newborn screening test to be developed using the dried-blood-spot technique and while it received the most recognition—many other tests have been developed using this same technique. These include biotin disorders, homocystinuria, congenital hypothyroidism, maple syrup urine disease, methylmalonic aciduria, histidinemia, sickle cell disease, galactokinase deficiency and transferase deficiency. Most of these disorders are characterized by progressive physical and mental degen-

eration. With the exception of sickle cell disease, they are all treatable by diet or medication. Untreated, those who suffer from these
disorders may develop seizures, some never learn to walk or talk and
become severely retarded. It would seem logical that physicians
would embrace these new advances in diagnostic techniques with
open arms; however, it has been a slow process to get many physicians to feel comfortable about routine biochemical screening techniques.

One venerable famous pediatrician, when asked about routine
screening, snorted in disgust, saying to his students, "We are trying
to teach you to be clinicians and not to be dependent upon any laboratory test." That concept might have seemed noble 40 years ago
when a blood count, tuberculin skin test and a test for syphilis were
the few routine laboratory studies performed. Today pediatricians
would be negligent if they did not routinely screen patients for a
variety of disorders that can be detected by blood and urine tests. It
has taken legislation to convince some doctors. In 1966, over the
objections of the California Medical Association, legislation was
passed in that state to test all newborn infants for PKU. The Medical Association argued that medical practice should not be legis-
lated. Since then, newborn screening has become standard practice
across the United States and in all developed countries.

Occasionally an infant with PKU is missed by screening procedures. In some cases the hospital has been at fault, mixing up the
records of infants; in rare cases records are lost; in other instances a
laboratory technician is at fault, misreading a test; or a doctor may
be at fault, not recognizing the importance of the test results. Since
a patient who is missed nearly always becomes retarded to some
extent and since PKU testing is now a standard of practice, nearly
all of these cases lead to malpractice suits. Most of these suits are
settled out of court and, to date, only one that went to trial has been
lost by the plaintiff.

Another complication affecting infant screening involves health
insurance companies. In many countries that have socialized medi-

cine, such as England, Germany and Canada, the phenylalanine-free medical food product is provided for PKU patients. Even so, some insurance companies and HMOs in the United States have refused to pay for the special food product for people with PKU. The excuse is that the product is a food and not a medication, so they have tried to relegate it to the same category as low-salt products for a person with high blood pressure or sugar-free products for a diabetic. These are feeble excuses: Patients with high blood pressure can easily eliminate salt from their diet without a special product; those with diabetes have many artificial sweeteners at their disposal; however, the person with PKU must have protein in order to live and grow, yet they cannot eat any protein-containing product available in the marketplace because all such products contain phenylalanine. A person with PKU must have the phenylalanine-free protein product to avoid suffering the resulting mental retardation.

The resistance on the part of insurance companies to paying for the product is understandable, as the diet is not inexpensive, costing some $5,000 per year. It has taken prodding by state health agencies and doctors, and sometimes threats of lawsuits, to challenge this policy. As an increasing number of children are diagnosed with disorders that require special medical food products, this policy will undoubtedly change, but it takes persistence to change the practices of insurance companies.

There are some exemplary screening programs throughout our country today: Massachusetts, for one, has a testing program in which all newborn babies are given blood tests to detect a number of different inherited diseases that cause mental retardation. In Pittsburgh Dr. Edwin Naylor is piloting a more complete testing program which can identify 20 to 30 different diseases on the blood spot obtained for newborn screening. Unfortunately, treatments have not been developed for all of the diseases that can be detected through screening. Niemann-Pick's Disease and Hurler's Disease are both hereditary disorders that cause progressive physical and mental degeneration. Children with these disorders usually do not live long.

The advantage of diagnosing these diseases is that couples who have had a child with one of these disorders would know the risk involved in having another and could be counseled about the advantages of prenatal diagnosis or the possibility of adoption as an alternative.

In addition to newborn screening the number of techniques available for achieving a reduction in the rate of mental retardation is still growing. It has taken a coalescing of medical advances and publicity to raise the awareness of the general public. In some cases legislation is necessary to ensure changes. Vaccines are now available to prevent most of the childhood diseases that in the past have lead to complications that could cause either death or mental retardation. Most states mandate that all children entering kindergarten be inoculated against measles, mumps and rubella. It is well known that a woman who contracts German measles (rubella) during the first three months of her pregnancy may bear a child with many handicaps, including mental retardation; therefore this immunization is especially important for girls. Unfortunately some people are unaware of the untold tragedies that result from unnecessary illness. Parents' organizations, in addition to the medical community, are waging campaigns to educate the public.

Certain disorders are more prevalent in particular ethnic groups. In January, 1974 California instituted a program to do mass screening of all ethnic Jews to detect carriers of Tay-Sachs Disease, a devastating hereditary disorder that strikes one out of every 3,600 infants whose parents are descended from Ashkenazi Jews. The disease is always fatal, with the infant deteriorating progressively, becoming blind, mentally retarded and ultimately dying between three to five years of age. The carriers are otherwise normal and usually have no idea they have a recessive gene for Tay-Sachs. It is only when two carriers have children that their offspring are vulnerable to the disease. For such a couple the odds are one out of four their children will have Tay-Sachs Disease, two out of four children will be carriers, and one out of four they will be completely unaffected. A test that is 100 percent accurate in detecting the carriers of this recessive disorder was developed by Dr. Michael Kaback in 1969. This allows carriers of the disorder to receive appropriate genetic counseling. The state of California has a population of a million ethnic Jewish people who have been helped by this screening program.

Premature birth can also cause mental retardation. The smaller and more immature an infant is at birth, the greater the chance it will not develop normally. Each year some 330,000 premature babies are born in the U.S.—about eight percent of all live births. In recent years the number of cerebral palsy cases has increased because, with improvements in the care of premature and low-birth-weight babies, more of them are surviving. Currently about 7,000 cases of cerebral palsy are diagnosed annually in the United States, a quarter of these cases occurring in infants weighing less than 3.3 pounds at birth.

Prematurity can occur when the mother is a hard drug user or smokes heavily during pregnancy. Smokers in our society often feel persecuted; however the dangers of smoking have been proven and are being well publicized. It is also important to realize that prematurity is often related to economic factors. The rate of prematurity is two to three times higher among women who have had little or no prenatal care and in poverty areas it is four to five times higher than in suburban areas.

One disturbing trend is the increasing number of babies born to teenage girls who often do not seek prenatal care. Typically they are single mothers who do not know how to care for an infant and are likely to live in poverty. Since prematurity and resulting mental retardation can be directly traced to poverty, every effort should be made to reduce the cost of health care so that everyone can afford it. Yet our national trend is in exactly the opposite direction. It seems incongruous that society is willing to pay for 30-year's care in an institution at $60,000 a year for each person with mental retardation, but is resistant to paying the comparatively small cost of good prenatal care and proper nutrition to prevent prematurity.

Reaching teenagers with the information they need in order to be responsible parents and citizens is a stubborn problem that has resisted many well-meaning efforts. The idea of having a cute little baby to love and cuddle appeals to some teenage girls who may feel they have very few options. So far, the advice to abstain or to practice safe sex has gone unheeded. Perhaps changes should be made in what is referred to as "sex education" in the public schools. One idea is to combine the curricula of sex education and health classes into a "family relations" class which would encompass not only sex education and health, but preventive medicine, prenatal care and drug education. It could even include balancing checking accounts and wise budgeting. Such a program might take away the stigma of the title "sex education" which is upsetting to some people and it would give young people a well-rounded fund of information that could be invaluable to them in later life.

It is now common knowledge that a well-balanced diet during pregnancy assists in the prevention of mental retardation in the fetus. Malnutrition is also a proven cause of mental retardation after a baby is born. A child who suffers from prolonged nutritional deprivation becomes weakened and cannot withstand the organisms to which it is exposed, leading to complications that can cause mental retardation. Protein deficiency, iron deficiency and vitamin B deficiency all can cause delayed development. Although these conditions are not often seen in the United States today, there are still hungry children in this country and malnutrition is a way of life in some developing countries.

Cretinism, a form of hypothyroidism caused by lack of iodine in the diet, was eradicated more than 50 years ago in developed countries where salt is iodized. It still exists in some countries such as India and the mountainous regions of Africa, Asia and South America. When he was in India, Bob Guthrie was told there are between one and ten million people suffering from cretinism there because of this problem. Prevention is easy and cheap. In 1990 the Prevention Committee of the International League of Societies for the Mentally Handicapped, chaired by Bob Guthrie, made several recommendations. The first was that cooking salt be iodized universally. The second was that all infants be immunized for a variety of diseases before leaving their place of birth. Even in industrialized countries approximately 25 percent of all newborns are not brought back at the optimal time for immunizations.

According to statistics reported at the 1995 International Council For Control of Iodine Deficiency Disorders (IDD) in Toronto, Canada, there are 1.6 billion people worldwide at risk for iodine deficiency disorders.

The United Nations, through the IDD, is actively engaged in eliminating this problem by instituting universal salt iodination and is already realizing some success. This problem could be completely eliminated by the year 2,000. Contributions by UNICEF and the World Bank have been most helpful.

Good prenatal care and obstetrical methods are readily available to women who seek them and can afford them. This now includes more than just appropriate nutrition and a monthly visit to the obstetrician's office so that the size and position of the fetus can be checked. It includes a test for rubella antibodies, as well as a test for the carrier status for Tay-Sachs Disease if the couple is Jewish. A careful review of the mother's medical history should rule out the possibility of maternal PKU and of diabetes mellitus. A woman with poorly controlled diabetes has an eight percent chance of producing an infant with congenital anomalies.

Rh factor is also important and should be determined by the obstetrician during a woman's first pregnancy. In those rare cases where the mother's blood is Rh negative and the father's is Rh positive, the pediatrician will be alerted to watch the newborn for signs of jaundice, the result of the mother's body developing antibodies to the positive Rh factor in the unborn infant's blood and destroying red blood cells. Unless a woman has had a blood transfusion at some time prior to her pregnancy, her body will not have built up these antibodies. However, during the pregnancy, sensitization to the Rh factor will occur, her body will react and future pregnancies will be at risk.

Severe jaundice can affect oxygen transport into the infant's brain cells and cause cerebral palsy; however, this is one of the causes of mental retardation that has been almost eliminated in developed countries. The drug Rhogam is now given to a woman with Rh negative blood after the birth of her first child to prevent antibody production against the Rh factor in future pregnancies. This procedure has virtually eliminated severe jaundice and exchange transfusions of newborns—conquering one more cause of mental retardation.

One form of mental retardation getting increased attention is fetal alcohol syndrome where the infant is damaged in utero by the mother's intake of alcohol. This is a preventable disorder in which the infant suffers microcephaly and facial dysmorphology, as well as mental retardation. There is now abundant publicity to warn prospective mothers about fetal alcohol. All containers of alcoholic beverages have the following printed warning on the labels, "According to the surgeon general, women should not drink alcoholic beverages during pregnancy because of the risk of birth defects."

In recent years doctors have been seeing an increasing number of children born addicted to drugs in utero. The problem of drug abuse is a persistent one that has yet to be solved, in spite of major efforts on the part of law enforcement agencies and drug education in the schools. In addition to causing premature births, this is adding to the numbers of children with attention deficit disorders and mental retardation. These children have great difficulty growing up to be contributing members of society since they cannot concentrate and learn easily.

As previously described, maternal PKU is another preventable cause of mental retardation. Women who have PKU and are off diet during pregnancy may have babies that are severely retarded. This has important implications for obstetricians; it is essential for them to determine the PKU status of their patients. Since the effects of diet discontinuation are quite slow in developing, these patients are sometimes unaware that they have a problem. Some women may remember having been on a special diet as a child, but not even know they had PKU.

There has been at least one malpractice lawsuit because an obstetrician did not realize the significance of the fact that his patient had PKU, even though she had told him about it and he had recorded it in her history. The patient had been off diet for a number of years and the obstetrician did not recognize the implications of the disorder. Her infant was needlessly and severely retarded. With the advent of maternal PKU camps and additional literature in the medical journals, this form of mental retardation should be declining.

Although it does not cause mental retardation, neuroblastoma is a disorder that is being diagnosed and treated in Japan. This is a type of cancer that can be successfully removed surgically if it is treated in the first year of life—and it can be detected with a urine test. Japan has a nationwide screening test for neuroblastoma that is collected on all six-month old infants. This test is somewhat controversial at present, as some surgeons in the United States feel that not all of the tumors diagnosed are malignant. The Japanese however feel the results justify the test. Perhaps this will become a standard of practice in developed countries in the future.

During the first three months of pregnancy before any immunities have been passed on to the fetus, it is especially vulnerable if the mother contracts certain infections. Toxoplasmosis is a disorder caused by a protozoan and is contracted by contact with the feces of cats and other animals. While it is not serious in adults, causing flu-like symptoms which are treatable with antibiotics, if a woman suffers toxoplasmosis during the first three months of pregnancy, it can cause intracranial calcification and mental retardation in the fetus. Pregnant women should delegate the emptying of cats' litter boxes to someone else. A skin test and the presence of toxoplasmosis antibodies will diagnose the disorder in an infant, but only after the brain has been damaged and treatment is of little value.

Cytomegalo virus infection is another disorder that can damage the fetus if contracted by the mother during the first three months of pregnancy. It also produces flu-like symptoms, but it is not sensitive to antibiotics. It can be diagnosed in an infant by culturing the urine for the virus. These disorders are rare, but the importance of a woman maintaining good health during pregnancy should be emphasized.

Every obstetrician is alert to the symptoms of toxemia, especially during the last three months of pregnancy. With toxemia the mother develops high blood pressure, albumin in the urine, dizzy spells and, in severe cases, convulsions. No one knows the cause of toxemia, but if the patient is put on a low salt diet and given medication for the high blood pressure, the symptoms are usually controlled. A new development in the treatment of toxemia is the use of the drug magnesium sulfate to control the symptoms. If this disorder is untreated the child is often born prematurely with an increased risk of mental retardation.

Good obstetrical methods are vitally important. A long, traumatic labor can lead to anoxia in the infant resulting in cerebral palsy. Placenta previa, in which the placenta separates from the uterine wall during the birth process, can also lead to brain damage. Since the placenta supplies food and oxygen to the fetus during the pregnancy and birth process, it must remain attached to the uterine wall until the baby breathes by itself. The experienced obstetrician can detect placenta previa, either by ultrasonography or physical examination, before the onset of labor and may decide to deliver the infant by Caesarean section. Although there has been criticism of doctors who perform too many Caesarean operations, for the most part these procedures are done for the health of the infant and not for the convenience of the doctor. A traumatic birth refers to any complication that can occur during delivery, such as a breech or transverse position of the baby, premature separation of the placenta or a very rapid or very long labor. These complications all require the skill of an experienced obstetrician.

The maternity nurse-practitioner has become an important member of the obstetrical team. This health professional can provide most of the prenatal care in uncomplicated cases, leaving the obstetrician more time to concentrate on the complicated cases that need special expertise. This program has been in operation for many years in the hills of Kentucky and Tennessee and has now been adopted by several other states.

Occasionally infants are born with serious defects that can be treated surgically, thus preventing mental retardation. With craniosynostosis the fissures of the infant's skull are fused together at birth. Instead of the infant having a fontanel or soft spot at the top of the head, making it possible for the head to contract during the birth process and leaving room for the rapid growth and expansion of its brain during the first year, some or all of the sutures in the skull have already fused by the time the baby is born. The skull cannot expand as the child's brain grows. There are a number of variations of this disorder. Sometimes only one or two of the sutures are fused and the head expands only where there are open fissures, producing an abnormal shape. Occasionally all the sutures are fused. With modern surgery, this is a form of mental retardation that no longer occurs in developed countries.

Other preventable causes of mental retardation are child abuse, unsafe equipment and environmental hazards. All medical personnel and others dealing with children are now required by law to report cases of suspected child abuse to the authorities. There are self-help organizations, as well as various forms of professional care available for abusive parents. In spite of all precautions, children still suffer skull fractures and other injuries from abuse that can cause mental retardation. Mental retardation is also caused by accidents. "Near drowning," where a child does not breathe for five to ten minutes can cause severe brain damage. All private and public swimming pools must now be fenced so that children cannot fall in accidentally. In spite of all such precautions, accidents still happen. Parents and child-care providers must always be alert. Even pails of water and toilets can and have caused the drowning and near drowning of small children.

Many states now require children riding bicycles to wear approved helmets to prevent skull fractures in case of accidents. In addition, legislation has been passed in most states requiring passengers in cars to be properly secured in approved car seats. Although some adults are resistant, motorcycle helmet laws and seat belt laws are saving lives and preventing injuries, many of which can cause brain damage. Statistics show that there are 50 percent fewer traumatic brain injuries in motorcycle crashes where a safety helmet is worn. In addition, states are now passing laws making it illegal for passengers to ride in the backs of pickup trucks where they are especially vulnerable. As discussed previously, a preventable form of mental retardation, lead poisoning, can also occur in a fetus, being passed on during pregnancy.

At the eighth International Symposium on Newborn Screening in Australia, Dr. Robert Elliot of New Zealand reported he had developed a screening test and treatment for juvenile or Type I diabetes. Although diabetes does not cause mental retardation, it is a serious illness and this announcement was greeted with optimism. Dr. Elliot reported that his test detects the circulating antibodies that destroy the insulin-producing cells in the pancreas. He performed his test on children five to seven years old and if a child had a positive result he administered nicotinamide to prevent diabetes from developing. Although this test and treatment are still controversial, research continues. If it proves reliable it will, indeed, be a major breakthrough.

Some people who have been very supportive of efforts to help persons with disabilities, have shied away from any discussion of prevention and genetic counseling because they feel that prevention automatically involves the divisive subject of abortion. As one can see from the foregoing, a great deal can be done to prevent mental retardation without abortion ever being discussed as an option. However, since the 1973 U.S. Supreme Court decision upholding a woman's right to terminate a pregnancy during the first six months, abortion is an alternative that is legally available to those who want it.

Although genetic counseling is thought of as a modern science, it has actually been practiced for hundreds of years. Going back to the twelfth and thirteenth centuries, the Talmud of the Jews specified that a person could not marry if epilepsy had occurred within his family during the past two generations. By custom in this country close relatives, such as first cousins, do not marry. The Religious Coalition on Reproductive Choice reports that, contrary to the beliefs of some, the Old and New Testaments contain no prohibitions against abortion. The Bible is silent on the subject, and the first recorded recipe for an abortifacient comes from the year 2600 BC.

Since a number of disorders can be prevented by termination of pregnancy in the early stages, the issue of abortion should be addressed. The decision to end a pregnancy is always a difficult one and should be the responsibility of the parents and their physician. It has been postulated that abortion can cause psychological damage and depression in a woman. In the 1980s Surgeon General C. Everett Koop conducted an extensive survey of women who had had abortions and found no widespread evidence of psychological breakdown or trauma resulting from the decision. In fact, it seems logical that a woman is more likely to suffer psychological damage and depression if she knows she is carrying a fetus with severe defects but is prevented from terminating the pregnancy.

The Catholic church has always been at the forefront of opposition to all mechanical and chemical forms of birth control, and teaches that abortion is not be condoned under any circumstances. In recent years there has been a divergence of opinion among Catholic theologians regarding the use of contraceptives. At present there is a trend among some Catholic clergy to "keep out of the bedroom." Many conscientious Catholic women are using the pill without opposition from their priests. Increasingly the church is emphasizing the importance of family planning and family planning counseling is available at some Catholic social service agencies.

Other churches, such as the Mormons and fundamentalist Christians are opposed in principle to limiting the size of a family merely for the convenience of the parents. These also oppose abortion. However there are few religions that would oppose the use of contraceptives to protect the mother's health or the use of abortion when the mother's life is in danger, in cases of incest, or to prevent the birth of a child with severe disabilities.

Since the Supreme Court decision on abortion there have been determined efforts to overturn or nullify it. Those who advocate an end to legalized abortion emphasize they are for the "right to life." For those who favor reproductive choice, quality of life is equally important. Once a child is born, that child has the right to live, no matter what abnormalities the child may have. In addition, children should have a right to a great deal more: the right to a nutritious diet and freedom from poverty and prejudice; the right to have deformities and abnormalities corrected through good medical care; the right not be locked up against their will in an institution; the right to develop to their fullest potential and the right to dignity and self-respect.

Techniques are now available to obstetricians that enable them to detect a number of severe disorders in utero. Ultrasound is a harmless procedure that can detect many problems such as heart defects, hydrocephaly (a form of brain damage) and anencephaly (absence of the brain) at an early stage of pregnancy. If there is a family history of genetic disorders or if anything seems abnormal about the pregnancy, an ultrasound picture will be performed as a precaution. Ultrasonography has become an invaluable addition to the arsenal of techniques used to detect various disorders.

Amniocentesis (obtaining a sample of amniotic fluid), cervical villous biopsy (biopsy of the early forming placenta) and cytogenetics (chromosome counting) are techniques used to detect Down syndrome in a fetus in the early stages of pregnancy. If a woman is over 35 years of age, or if there is a family history of genetic disorders, amniocentesis and cytogenetic studies will usually be ordered. This involves obtaining a sample of amniotic fluid by a needle puncture guided by ultrasound through the abdominal wall into the uterus. There are always enough free-floating fetal cells in the fluid to provide an adequate sample to be examined in the laboratory. The usual test is for chromosome disorders, but testing can also be done for Tay-Sachs Disease. Since it has become common knowledge that Down syndrome is caused by an extra number 21 chromosome in each body cell, the technique of cytogenetics has become invaluable in detecting this and other chromosome disorders. This can be done in the twelfth to sixteenth week of pregnancy.

Some of the newer medical discoveries include the ability to detect neural tube defects in utero. These are serious disorders in which there is a blockage of the cerebrospinal fluid that is manufactured in the choroid plexus in the central part of the brain. Above and below the choroid plexus are cavities or ventricles. The cerebrospinal fluid normally circulates in the ventricles of the brain and down the spinal cord where it then travels up the outside of the brain. It is thought by some that a large portion of the fluid is absorbed by the gray matter or the cortex.

If the flow of cerebrospinal fluid is blocked, pressure builds up in the ventricles of the brain eventually causing the skull to enlarge in a condition called hydrocephalus, literally meaning water on the brain. There are two forms of hydrocephalus: obstructive and communicating. In obstructive hydrocephalus the canal carrying the fluid becomes blocked near the base of the brain. Sometimes the cause of this obstruction is present at birth, but it can also be caused by meningitis, brain tumor or birth injury. This can be diagnosed in an infant by injecting a dye through the fontanel into a ventricle of the brain and then performing a spinal tap. If there is no obstruction, the dyed fluid should circulate to the cite of the spinal tap within a few minutes. If no fluid containing dye is obtained in the tap, the diagnosis of obstructive hydrocephalus can be made. This can be treated surgically by connecting a small tube above and below the obstruction so that it is bypassed. In the communicating form of hydrocephalus there is no obstruction. It is believed that when the fluid reaches the brain cortex, it is not properly absorbed and eventually collects in the ventricles. The treatment involves the placing of a small tube leading from one of the ventricles of the brain to the large vessel leading to the heart (the superior vena cava). The excess fluid is drained away into the bloodstream. This procedure is called a ventriculocardiac shunt.

Spina bifida is another form of neural tube disorder which is caused by a congenital defect involving the spine. In spina bifida there is a distortion in the alignment of the spinal column, with the vertebrae actually forming a curve or loop. Attached to this spinal derangement is a pouch of cerebrospinal fluid and spongy tissue called a meningiomyelocele from which some of the cerebrospinal fluid escapes. This tissue can be removed surgically, but not always successfully. Sometimes the fluid that was escaping is blocked after surgery, resulting in hydrocephalus or the spinal nerves are damaged by the defect, resulting in paraplegia, loss of bladder and rectal control and loss of sensation in the lower extremities.

An elevated level of alpha feto-protein in the blood is a warning to the physician to rule out the presence of neural tube defect in the fetus and an ultrasound would be ordered. On the other hand, a low level of alpha feto-protein is a sign that the fetus may have Down syndrome and an amniocentesis would be ordered. A recent discovery indicates that a diet low in folic acid, a component of the vitamin B complex, can cause spina bifida. Therefore all good prenatal nutritional advice emphasizes that a woman take 400 mcg of folic acid per day—a cheap insurance against a devastating disorder.

For some people the termination of pregnancy to prevent the birth of a child with a severe disability is considered a life-saving measure. If it were not for the option of abortion, a couple producing a child with a severe disability might never have another child. In years past, this was often the case. Such couples were deprived of the pleasure of raising healthy, nonhandicapped children because of the fear they would produce another one with disabilities. Thanks to the development of the techniques now available to detect these defects during the early stages of pregnancy and the availability of legal, safe abortion, many children who would never have been conceived in former years are actually living today. High-risk couples are increasingly using these methods of guaranteeing that their child will not have a severe form of mental handicap.

It should be added that abortion should never be forced upon anyone. If a fetus is found to be abnormal, genetic counseling should be offered. But the decision must be left to the couple involved. Should the couple decide against abortion, their decision must be respected, with the assurance that they will receive moral support and their child will receive the best of medical care.

It takes hard work by many people to make progress in the prevention of mental retardation: by parents who want the best for their children and who sometimes have to demand that their needs be met; by researchers who have made so many discoveries; by lawmakers who have enacted legislation mandating certain practices such as newborn screening, seat belts, infant safety seats, bicycle helmets, and more; and by medical professionals such as doctors, nurses, and nutritionists.

We must remember that the prevention of a single case of mental retardation saves society about a million dollars, in addition to relieving that family of the burdens of grief and suffering. For many years, Bob Guthrie was chair of the Prevention Committee of the Association of Retarded Citizens, a position now held by Peter Leibert, who produces a monthly newsletter on prevention of mental retardation which highlights the latest information on the subject. He also lets his readers know about new proposed legislation in the field of prevention.

Interested subscribers can receive this newsletter for an annual donation of $15 sent to ARC-California, 120 I Street, Sacramento, CA 95814.

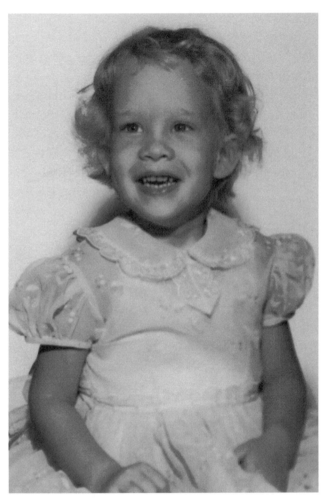

Margaret Doll, aged 3, Bob Guthrie's niece with PKU who one year was the Minnesota March of Dimes poster child.

13

Profiles of Patients with PKU

Margaret Doll

Margaret Doll was born July 2, 1958. Her mother, Mary Lou, is Margaret Guthrie's sister and the baby was named after her aunt and a grandmother. Margaret Doll was the first child in the family and her parents were pleased to have a normal, healthy infant. Her mother nursed her and she was a happy, responsive baby. She babbled and cooed and reached for objects just as Dr. Spock's baby care book said she should. Although she was a little slow in the development of motor skills, Dr. Spock indicated that children vary in this regard.

When she was about seven months old, Margaret became more subdued and began to drop her head. Mary Lou was concerned and talked with the doctor. He asked her about the baby's developmental milestones, but did not do the PKU diaper test. When Margaret was nine months old, the doctor referred them to a pediatrician who did a thorough examination. He, too, omitted the diaper test, even though he had recently attended a presentation on PKU and had seemed quite interested in the disorder.

He said that Margaret was "somewhat retarded" and the slight head dropping might be small seizures. He recommended a brain wave test at the university, although there was no hurry as she was very young for specific results. Mary Lou took a brochure from the Association for Retarded Children that was in the doctor's office and contacted the organization. She had already heard about the organization from her brother-in-law, Bob Guthrie. Later she and her husband, Orval, became active members.

Mary Lou contacted Bob about her worries regarding Margaret's slow development when she was about a year old. He referred the Dolls to the University of Minnesota for a more thorough evaluation. When the diaper test was finally done, it was positive. Ironically Bob Guthrie's niece, his wife's namesake, had PKU.

Margaret did not start the special diet until she was thirteen months old, as the PKU specialist at the university was out of the country until then. She was always good about her diet, even eating the Lofenelac powder dry with a spoon. Margaret rolled over at 15 months, sat up at 18 months, walked at 27 months and started saying words at three years. She was taken off the diet when she was eight, as most pediatricians were doing at that time. At the present time, however, most doctors in this field feel it is preferable to continue the diet for life.

When she was taken off the diet Margaret had an IQ of 25. Her psychologist thought she was able to concentrate better when she was on diet, so she did go back on the diet for a year or two, but her parents found the regimen increasingly difficult to maintain. They weighed the value of the diet against the social problems she encountered because of it and decided to discontinue it. She already had severe mental retardation and her parents felt the pleasure she derived from normal food was more important in her life than the powers of concentration.

Margaret seemed happy and coöperative. Over the years she went to several special schools and did well, learning from parallel play and copying others. Each summer she went to a camp for children with disabilities. She enjoyed music and singing and her record player was her pride and joy. Physically she had no problems and her parents took her everywhere with them.

Mary Lou and Orval never had any other children because of the fear that they might have another child with PKU, but when Margaret was four, they started caring for foster children. She responded well to them and they accepted her as a regular member of the family. By this time the Dolls had become active in the ARC and had many friends in the organization. One year Margaret was selected as the poster child by the March of Dimes, Minnesota chapter.

When Margaret was ten, the Dolls were asked by friends if they would consider taking care of their mentally disabled child for a weekend. Mary Lou and Orval accepted and that was how they became involved in respite care. The dedicated people who do respite care deserve special recognition. Often these people make it possible for a family to keep a child with disabilities at home rather than be faced with the wrenching option of institutionalization. The Dolls have kept children for up to ten days at a time. Although Orval passed away in 1989, Mary Lou still continues doing respite care.

Mary Lou and Orval also provided shelter care for abandoned, neglected children, and were on call day and night. If they had an empty bed and a child was in need, they put them up. On some occasions they kept these children for six months to a year. Mary Lou felt all of the children seemed to learn from each other. Later she and Orval legally adopted three of the nondisabled boys in their care.

When Margaret was 21, her behavior began to change—and the changes came rapidly. Within a few months she developed sleep disturbances and would wake up screaming at night. She started throwing clothes and furniture. Lights and noise bothered her. In the daytime she needed more space. She would hit the other children if they walked too close to her, then accuse them of hitting her or spilling her milk. She talked to unseen persons and stared off into space, smiling for unknown reasons. The doctor said these were psychotic manifestations and he prescribed mellaril.

The Dolls finally had to place Margaret in a group home, where she became increasingly difficult to manage. She was aggressive, especially when anyone tried to get her up in the morning. Her medication made her lethargic and she had crying jags for no apparent reason. At one point she was given lithium, which stopped the crying jags but it made her hair fall out. Without her medication she was unmanageable, breaking windows, beating herself on the head or chest, banging her head on the wall, even hitting the driver while riding in a car. Finally the group home personnel could no longer deal with her and the Dolls had to find another facility.

Unfortunately, despite the abundance of group homes in Minnesota, Margaret no longer fit into the docile, passive pattern of behavior expected at most of them. Her doctor prescribed a mood elevator and inderal in addition to the mellaril. Margaret is now in her fourth group home and seems to be doing well—as long as she is on her medication. She has also gone back on the low-phenylalanine diet, this time successfully. The formula is more tasty than it was originally and more products have been developed to supplement the diet. There was a marked improvement in Margaret's behavior when she went back on the diet. The home where Margaret lives is a small one with only four residents, all of them with behavior problems, all of them lower functioning than Margaret. She likes to work in the kitchen, peeling potatoes, opening cans, and other such tasks. Otherwise she is sedentary, although food is a great motivator.

Margaret has a good relationship with members of the staff. They fix her hair, do her nails and take her to dances. She likes to bowl and scores 70 to 80, sometimes higher. And she still loves music and can carry a tune. It may take a bit of persuasion to get her to go biking, but she can ride a two-wheeler well. Mary Lou takes her home or takes her out for a meal about every third weekend. They go bowling if it is not too crowded and they go to church together. Margaret shakes hands with people and says, "Hi, how are you today?"

Mary Lou feels that Margaret's life has been a motivating factor, for because of her the family started taking in foster children. Margaret's presence helped the other children in their home learn to accept and understand those who were different. It was because of Margaret that Mary Lou and Orval became involved in the ARC, eventually doing respite and shelter care. Perhaps most important, because of Margaret, her Uncle Bob redoubled his efforts to develop a newborn screening test for PKU. She played a part in hastening the development of this test that has spared untold numbers of families the grief her parents endured.

The Dolls made a profound difference in their community, especially for children—those with disabilities as well as the non-disabled. When Orval Doll passed away in 1989 his obituary in the local paper referred to him as the "father" of 225 children. Except for Margaret, they were all foster children.

Kathy and David

Kathy H. was born in 1947, her parents' first child. She was rather irritable as a baby, but did not appear to have any disabilities. She had diarrhea much of the time and was slow in achieving her developmental milestones. Mrs. H. questioned her doctor about Kathy's development, but he did not seem concerned, saying she was just slow. As she got older Kathy was active and volatile and her parents were unable to toilet-train her. For a while she attended nursery school, giving her mother some respite.

When Kathy was five, her brother David was born. From the beginning, he was irritable and he too was slow in developing. Again, the doctor did not seem to be concerned. When David was two, the H. family visited relatives in New York. While they were there David was so irritable they took him to New York Hospital where he was admitted. One of the diagnostic tests was the ferric chloride diaper test for PKU and it was positive. Kathy was subsequently diagnosed with PKU too.

The family was referred to Childrens Hospital in Los Angeles where the children were seen by a doctor who specialized in metabolic disorders. Unfortunately, Kathy and David were diagnosed in 1954—before there were any dietary products available commercially for children with PKU. Working with nutritionists and biochemists, the doctors at Childrens Hospital ordered the ingredients for a formula that Mrs. H. could prepare at home. She was given a supply of oil, sugar, tyrosine and other chemicals, and she bought a scale so that she could measure each ingredient accurately. She then had to cook the mixture which became the consistency of pudding. It tasted terrible and the children refused to eat it, but Mr. and Mrs. H. persevered. Each day Mrs. H. tested the children's urine with ferric chloride to see if it turned green, indicating that they were eating too much phenylalanine. The children continued to refuse the food and, after two frustrating years, David became malnourished and had to be hospitalized. In frustration Mr. and Mrs. H. gave up the diet.

When David turned five, a commercial product became available and he and Kathy were again put on the diet. Neither of them would take the formula and after two more years of trying, the parents again gave up the diet. In spite of the enormous amount of work involved in caring for the children, Mr. and Mrs. H. kept them at home until Kathy was 17 and David was 13. At that time they placed them at Pacific State Hospital for the Mentally Retarded (now called Lanterman Developmental Center). Kathy had never become toilet-trained and continued to be very active. David was quiet and easier to manage, but neither he nor Kathy learned to talk.

Mr. and Mrs. H. feel the children have had good care at Lanterman. For a while they brought them home frequently for overnight visits. This became increasingly difficult and they now visit the children every other weekend at Lanterman instead. David and Kathy recognize them and are always happy to see them. Kathy is still hyperactive and aggressive. As her mother says, "She is a screamer." She does not like being touched, becoming self-abusive and breaking windows when she is upset. She has banged her head so much that her forehead is permanently disfigured, and her physical strength makes it difficult to care for her. At one time she was put back on the diet as the staff hoped her behavior might improve, but she refused the formula again. Her weight finally reached a low of 80 pounds and Mrs. H. asked that she be taken off diet.

Kathy is now 45 years old, has severe osteoporosis and has broken her hips so many times she can no longer walk normally. She wears a brace on her left leg and a lift on one shoe and is in a wheel chair most of the time. She is unable to chew so she gets a soft diet. She is a picky eater and although she can feed herself with difficulty, members of the staff usually feed her. In spite of all her problems, Kathy is aware of her surroundings and has a lot of pluck. Mrs. H. notes that if she does something she knows is naughty, like throwing something on the floor, she will look up and laugh.

David is still quiet and lovable, not as responsive as Kathy. When he becomes irritated, he slaps himself in the face. Kathy and David go to "school" five days a week where they practice some skills. They do exercises to increase their coördination—finger painting and filling bottles with water. David especially likes school because they are taken there on a tram—which delights him.

Kathy and David have no friends at Lanterman and on the weekends there is nothing for them to do. Mr. and Mrs. H. have a good relationship with the members of the staff and they appreciate their dedication to a difficult job. A pharmacist is working with the doctors to reduce the amount of medication used on the residents and Mr. and Mrs. H. are pleased with this. They feel the hospital is understaffed, but that the state facilities are improving. It saddens them to see some of the residents, whose families have simply "warehoused" them at the facility and never visit them.

Although Kathy and David were born too long ago to be helped, Mr. and Mrs. H. have become actively involved as volunteers one day a week at the PKU clinic at Childrens Hospital. Mrs. H. also volunteers at a hospital gift shop. It pleases them to see the progress of other young people who have PKU, children growing up without disabilities because of prompt diagnosis and treatment. It gives them a sense of pride to know that they are part of the team at the PKU clinic.

Nickelle W. and her Mother

Nickelle W. is 14, the second in a family of four children. Her father is a pharmacist, planning to get his Ph.D., and her mother is a medical transcriber. This account is the result of interviews with Nickelle and her mother while Nickelle was in the hospital for observation, testing and evaluation of her potential for staying on the PKU phenylalanine-restricted diet. She has been out of control for at least the past two years.

Nickelle was diagnosed at birth with PKU. Her parents lived in the northwest and were referred to the PKU clinic at the University of Washington where they received a lot of moral support and help. They attended a parent support group where they met with other parents of children with PKU. There was a great team of professionals, including a psychologist, nutritionist and pediatrician at the clinic who were able to answer questions. This made it easier to accept the fact that the baby they had planned for had a disorder that would require a great deal of special care throughout her lifetime.

The support sessions were for the parents at first, but soon the children were included. When they were old enough to read the words "yes" and "no," they were told about "yes foods" and "no foods" and given pictures of foods, like a banana or an egg, and instructed to color the "yes food" but not the "no food." When the children got older, a nutritionist held cooking classes for them where they learned to prepare foods low in phenylalanine. Nickelle was taught from an early age to select foods that would not harm her.

In spite of all the support Nickelle's mother says she herself felt overwhelmed and chronically tired. Although her husband was supportive of her emotionally, he did none of the actual physical work of the household or figuring the appropriate amounts of various foods or preparing meals. Mrs. W. had a written schedule for feedings when Nickelle was an infant: eight a.m.—give eight ounces of formula, nine a.m.—give eight ounces apple juice, and so on. In spite of this meticulous planning the baby seemed to be constantly hungry. At the age of six months, for a period of six weeks, Nickelle did not thrive and gained no weight at all. Out of desperation, and against the advice of the nutritionist, Mrs. W. started her on some low-protein solid foods. Nickelle started to gain some weight and was happier.

When Nickelle was two years old, a new baby was born to Mrs. W. and two years later another baby completed the family. Mrs. W. describes her feelings of anger, guilt and frustration. She never really had time to reflect on these feelings because she was so busy just doing what she had to do to keep the family going, taking care of routine household chores, keeping everyone on the proper schedule, packing special lunches for Nickelle to carry to school each day and preparing two separate meals each evening.

In 1989 Mr. W. joined the military and the family moved to another state where Mrs. W. took a job outside the home. Mr. and Mrs. W. took Nickelle to the local PKU clinic, but did not experience the support they had felt in Washington. The clinic director was rather quiet and soft-spoken and the parents missed the strong support team they had in Washington.

Since Mrs. W. was now working outside the home and as she felt Nickelle was old enough to take more responsibility for her own diet, Nickelle was left with little supervision and was expected to make appropriate choices for herself. Although she always appeared to be staying on her diet when she was at home, it seemed she had started "cheating" as her phenylalanine levels rose. This was even more upsetting and frustrating to Mrs. W., who was so busy and overwhelmed with family responsibilities.

When Nickelle was twelve, Mr. W. was transferred to a different base and the family moved again. Mr. and Mrs. W. have always been fortunate in that their medical insurance carrier and, later, the military paid for the phenylalanine-free formula. But by this time Nickelle was almost completely off diet, still going through the pretense of being on it in the presence of her family. She would often "forget" to take her phenylalanine-free medical food until she was reminded by her mother. On one occasion, Mrs. W. waited to see how long it would be before she would remember; but at the end of five days, she reminded her.

Nickelle would mix her day's supply of formula each morning and was supposed to finish it by that evening. One problem her mother noticed was that the formula powder would go into solution and quickly sink to the bottom of the container. With its rather chalky, disagreeable taste, Nickelle developed the habit of "forgetting" to shake it up before drinking it. She ended up just drinking the water at the top and the nutritious part of the formula was left in the bottom of the container to be washed down the drain at the end of the day.

Nickelle began having problems at school with peer pressure. Other children would ask why she was ordering hamburgers without meat in them, although no one actually teased her about her odd eating habits. Nickelle did not tell many of her friends that she had PKU. In fact, she did not have many friends, being tired and cranky much of the time. Low self-esteem, poor grades and, according to Mrs. W., an attitude problem with some of her teachers added to her difficulties. She would come home from school each day so tired she would sleep until dinner time and, after dinner, go back to sleep. Mrs. W. was increasingly alarmed. She had always subscribed to the PKU newsletter and knew Nickelle's diet should be under more control. She knew Nickelle was angry about the diet, about having PKU, and often angry at her parents, although she was never able to admit her anger.

Finally Mr. and Mrs. W. heard about a local doctor who worked with PKU patients. During their appointment with her, to their consternation she was nonchalant about the diet, saying it was nothing to be concerned about. When Mrs. W. questioned her about the research findings and maternal PKU, issues reported in the PKU newsletter, she said there were two ways of looking at the problem and she did not consider the diet to be that important. Nickelle's parents did not return for a second appointment.

The year before Nickelle entered high school there were increasing problems in school. Mrs. W. had a conference with the assistant principal and, almost as an afterthought, she told him, "It probably isn't important, but Nickelle has PKU. I don't know whether that has anything to do with her problems." She half expected him to ask what PKU was. Instead, he said he thought it just might have something to do with her problems. His cousin's husband was a specialist in PKU at Childrens Hospital in Los Angeles. He gave her the doctor's name and phone number.

Mrs. W. talked with the doctor by phone and they decided that she should bring Nickelle to the hospital for a stay of five days for a thorough evaluation. They had to get special permission from their health insurance carrier. But after a minimum of red tape, they received it and Nickelle and her mother came to Childrens Hospital. Mrs. W. stayed at the local Ronald McDonald House while Nickelle was in the hospital.

Nickelle was put on a phenylalanine-restricted diet and given the phenylalanine-free product each day. She was seen by a psychologist who found that she was above average in intelligence. A nutritionist met with her and introduced a new orange-flavored diet product. Mrs. W. liked it because it went into solution and stayed in solution so it did not have to be shaken up. Nickelle did not care for the flavor, preferring her old formula with coffee to disguise the taste. Mrs. W. thought she should at least try the new product for a while, as it is a more complete formula.

While she was in the hospital Nickelle and her mother had a frank discussion about her feelings about having PKU. Mrs. W. told her it was okay to feel bad and angry. For the first time in her life, Nickelle cried openly about it. When Nickelle was interviewed she seemed rather quiet and did not elaborate much in her responses—until the interviewer mentioned that she had heard she was an artist. Immediately Nickelle brightened and displayed a few of her drawings, which, indeed, showed artistic talent. She said she realized she was "different" when she was five or six years old, but did not try to explain about PKU to many of her friends or teachers. They just thought she didn't like to eat certain foods. Often she went home for lunch, rather than taking it to school. When she was invited to parties, her mother always prepared her own piece of cake. She admitted that she is angry about having PKU and that she can't eat what her friends eat. At times she was angry at her parents, too.

Nickelle has become acquainted with at least two other young women who have PKU. They are both older than Nickelle, but she enjoys being with them. One is married and has two children. Having stayed on the diet during her pregnancies, neither of her children are disabled. The other woman is a social worker who lives about an hour away. She and Nickelle have gotten together for a few social occasions and they are exchanging recipes. This young woman has attended maternal PKU camp for several summers which she found to be a positive experience. She is encouraging Nickelle to go with her next summer and Nickelle is looking forward to this with some excitement.

In high school Nickelle's grades continue to be poor. She loves art, physical education, drivers' education and socializing. She hates math, typing and Spanish. She is particularly "bugged" by tests, as she has trouble concentrating that long. Once she is back on diet, she thinks she will be able to focus and concentrate better. During the lunch hour at school she usually just has a soda and "hangs out," then eats when she gets home. Nickelle does not belong to any clubs at school and most of her social outlets are through her church. There are activities for teenagers there on Sunday and Wednesday evenings and a drama club which she really enjoys. There are also field trips, like going to Disneyland. Nickelle talks as though she definitely plans to stick to her diet. She does not know whether she will have more energy when she is on diet, but she is going to see.

Although she is definitely drawn to art, Nickelle believes she would like to become a model some day and is looking into a few modeling schools. When told that her hair would probably get darker after she went on the diet, she lamented, "Oh, no. I like my blond hair." Last summer she was a junior life guard and her hair became sun-bleached. She is looking forward to the same bonus this summer. In the meantime, she is inspired to stay on the diet.

The results of Nickelle's tests show an IQ of 110 on the Wechsler Intelligence Test for Children. Her EEG is normal; however, the MRI scan of her brain shows demyelinization extending into the optic radiation. Her blood phenylalanine level is 26 mg percent (high). Her tyrosine level is 0.51 mg (low). Blood chemistry, complete blood count and urinalysis are all normal. The psychiatric evaluation indicates mild depression.

When Nickelle leaves the hospital a phenylalanine-restricted diet plus a phenylalanine-free food product will be prescribed in addition to 500 mg of tyrosine two times per day. Her blood phenylalanine level will be monitored monthly until it is under control. After that it will be monitored quarterly. The doctor is hopeful that, if she sticks to the phenylalanine-restricted diet and takes her phenylalanine-free product getting her phenylalanine levels under control, she will have more energy, feel better and be able to concentrate longer in school.

Pinky

The story of Pinky is heartwarming, especially in these times when much of our available medical care seems impersonal and government agencies seem bound by bureaucracy. It actually begins before Pinky was born and before the Guthrie test had been developed and involves Dr. Willard (Bill) Centerwall, the PKU pioneer who developed the diaper test. Dr. Centerwall and his wife, Siegried, also a physician, went to India as medical missionaries from 1961 to 1966. While there Bill was contacted by U.S. government personnel who asked him to begin a country-wide PKU testing program in the hospital maternity wards, not realizing that the vast majority of infants in India were not born in hospitals and thus such a program would be of no value.

The next request was that he obtain urine specimens from every patient in every institution for persons with developmental disabilities in the country to administer his ferric chloride test on them. There were then 26 known small institutions in India with a total enrollment of 1,276 persons. Bill Centerwall reports that he spent three weeks traveling the length and breadth of the country by every possible conveyance, even wading across a water-submerged bridge over a flood-swollen river in Dehra Dun in the foothills of the Himalayas to reach all of the institutions.

Through his testing he found two unrelated children, a boy and a girl, who had PKU. The boy had a sister at home who had developmental disabilities. When she was tested, she was also found to have PKU. Both sets of parents were notified of the diagnosis and informed that the disorder was hereditary. Shortly before the Centerwalls were due to return home from India, the mother of the two children with PKU became pregnant. By this time Bob Guthrie had developed his dried-blood-spot test so Bill Centerwall asked him for a kit so that a blood spot could be collected from the baby when it was born and returned to Bob's lab to be tested for PKU. Before leaving India, Bill Centerwall contacted the family's physician and left him the test kit and a supply of phenistix (ferric chloride impregnated paper strips) that had been donated by the Ames Company in the United States to be used for PKU testing of the infant's urine.

Dr. Centerwall also wrote to the Mead Johnson Company in the U.S. and they agreed to supply the special formula for the infant at no cost in case the diagnosis was positive. Then he contacted the Health Minister of the government of India who arranged to have such a brain-protecting diet product, if needed, imported into the country duty-free. The health minister also arranged to have a local physician of the Indian government provide monitoring, guidance and care for the child if it did have PKU.

When the baby was born it was a girl and, indeed, the test was positive. So began the longest distance care of a PKU case ever recorded, a uniquely multinational venture. A monthly dried-blood spot on filter paper was mailed to Bob's lab in Buffalo, New York, and the results were mailed back to the locally-placed government doctor in India. The local professionals were then able to communicate with the family and to adjust the diet, as indicated by the test results. The Mead Johnson Company continued to provide the medical product and the child progressed nicely.

Bob met Pinky, as she was always called, on his first trip to India in March 1985 when she was 17. Although her phenylalanine-restricted diet had been discontinued when she was just past five, she was doing well on a typical Indian vegetarian diet. At that meeting she was dressed in pink and Bob assumed that was because her nickname was Pinky. Her parents later told Dr. Centerwall she was called Pinky because of her naturally light, pink complexion—the result of her PKU. Her international medical team did its job well and she grew up to be an attractive young woman without any of the complications of untreated PKU.

Pinky married a physician in India—an ear, nose and throat specialist. At that time she was told she should go on a strict phenylalanine-restricted diet along with a medical protein food product before planning to have a baby. By that time Bob Guthrie had retired so Dr. Harvey Levy at the Massachusetts State Screening Lab agreed to monitor her phenylalanine levels, with advice and consultation from Dr. Centerwall, now in Oregon, and Pat Portnoi with Scientific Hospital Supplies in Liverpool, England. She did become pregnant, but despite all of the concern of her family and her international team, she did not get her phenylalanine under control until well into the first trimester of her pregnancy.

Bill Centerwall was scheduled to visit India in the fall of 1995 and an important part of his agenda was to visit Pinky, her husband and the new baby. As it happened, he was present at the hospital when her baby was born. She had a little boy who appeared healthy and normal at first but by the second day the doctors could hear a serious heart murmur, one of the complications that can occur in a baby when the mother has PKU and is off diet during pregnancy.

This story finally had a happy ending, however. Surgery was successful and the baby is now a healthy toddler.

Susan M.

Susan was born in 1960. Her mother was a teacher. Her father taught at the college level and owned a private art gallery. She seemed normal at birth and her medical care was provided by her grandfather, a doctor. As an infant her food did not seem to agree with her and she vomited frequently. In addition, she was slow in achieving her developmental milestones. She would bang her head when she was frustrated and developed the mannerism of fluttering her hands. At that time the diaper test for PKU was being used by a few pediatricians and at some university-affiliated medical centers, but Susan's grandfather was in general practice and had not read about PKU.

Finally Mrs. M. enrolled Susan in nursery school at a child study center, a facility for children with emotional disturbances, even though Susan's only problems were slow development and a lack of verbal skills. One day at the Center a doctor did the PKU test on Susan, placing a few drops of ferric chloride on her wet diaper. As Mrs. M. watched the procedure she was surprised to see the spot turn bright green, indicating that Susan was excreting phenylketones in her urine. Susan was referred to a specialist at a southland university for treatment.

The specialist examined Susan and declared her to be "retarded." Mr. and Mrs. M. were told they could keep her in their home for a few years if they wished, but they should be prepared for her to grow up in an institution. He did not refer her to a nutritionist, but he did put her on a low-protein diet. On a follow-up her blood phenylalanine levels were found to be 14 to 20 instead of the normal three to eight. Upset that Susan's levels were so high, Mrs. M. went to the library and read everything she could find about PKU. She was so persistent in calling the doctor with her worries that he finally became impatient with her and told her not to bother him any more.

Mrs. M. finally told her father-in-law about her concerns and her frustration. He had practiced medicine in New York before coming to California. Although he knew nothing about PKU, he checked with some of his former colleagues there and ultimately referred her to Dr. George Jervis. Mrs. M. took Susan to his facility at Letchworth Village, New York, where he did a thorough examination. Susan was still unable to talk and was also developmentally retarded. Dr. Jervis believed she had a chance and referred her to a specialist at the Childrens Hospital of Los Angeles.

As soon as she returned from New York, Mrs. M. got an appointment for Susan at the PKU clinic at Childrens Hospital. She was asked to keep a record of everything Susan ate for three days before coming in for the appointment. The doctor examined her and Mrs. M. was interviewed by a nutritionist who was horrified at the foods Susan had been eating. She was two when she was put on Lofenalac. She did not like it, but her mother persisted and Susan was a coöperative child.

Susan started talking when she was three. Her mother enrolled her at a community center nursery school and she made progress. When she was five, she attended another school for children with emotional problems which led to further improvement. At the age of nine she entered the fourth grade at a private school and was mainstreamed into regular classes. She remained there until she finished high school. Susan always stayed at grade level, getting Cs and Bs and some As. She did find high school math to be difficult for her.

Mr. and Mrs. M. had decided not to have any other children because of the possibility that they would have another child with PKU, but when it became possible to do prenatal diagnosis of PKU, the doctor who had cared for Susan suggested that if they wanted another child they would not have to fear having another one with PKU. Mrs. M. subsequently became pregnant and a beautiful girl was born—without PKU.

In the early 1970s, when Susan was ten, following their standard practice at that time, the doctors at the PKU clinic told her she would not have to be on the diet indefinitely and could go off diet if she wished. Her mother objected. She felt that Susan was doing so well she should not take such a risk. She felt the diet was more important than social considerations or the slight inconvenience involved, so Susan stayed on diet and carried her lunch to school every day. Over the years she tried several different products. Some, like Albumaid, tasted terrible; some were not too bad. She thought the best was Phenylfree.

After graduating from high school, Susan took some nursing courses and did quite well. She had an excellent memory for details. Ultimately she earned an AA degree in Early Childhood Education and worked at a community center nursery school for five years. In 1987, when Susan became engaged, she and her fiance made an appointment at the PKU clinic for counseling. The doctor explained that if a woman with PKU is off diet and becomes pregnant, it is highly likely that her baby will have serious disabilities, such as heart problems and microcephaly. He recommended that if they planned to have children Susan should come in for a checkup and make sure her levels were within normal range before becoming pregnant.

When Susan and her husband decided the time had come to start a family they again called the clinic. Susan went on a strict diet so that her levels were very low. She was assured that if she maintained her diet during the pregnancy there was little likelihood that she would have a baby with disabilities. Her baby girl was born in late October of 1989. At birth the baby's cord-blood phenylalanine was 5.2 mg percent. She is a bright, beautiful, normal baby. In 1992 Susan entered the same profession as her mother, teaching at the same private school that she attended as a student. Mrs. M. feels that having Susan made her a better, more understanding teacher. Susan's doctors feel that she is an ideal testimonial to the proper management of PKU.

Newborn Screening for Sickle Cell Disease

by Kenneth A. Pass

Background

For much of the 20th century, investigations into sickle cell disease and sickle hemoglobin have served as a standard-bearer in genetics research. From the first suggestion of a link between the observed changes in red cells of anemic individuals, to description of the amino acid substitution within the DNA molecule directing synthesis of sickle hemoglobin, milestones of genetic progress have been marked with discoveries in sickle cell research. J.B. Herrick described in 1910 the peculiar sickled cells in a blood smear of a Granadian dental student suffering from anemia, which he related to a painful crisis subsequently experienced by the student. Interestingly (at least with today's perspective) Herrick never made much of the observation, moving instead into cardiovascular research; and the student is reported to have died at an early age, perhaps of pneumonia related to his sickle cell disease. Other observation of red cells sickling in low oxygen conditions followed in 1917 in a wet sealed preparation and more definitively in 1927 when Gillespie demonstrated the dependency of sickling on low oxygen pressures. By 1940 it was recognized that laboratory demonstration of red cell sickling could be induced in blood from anemic patients more readily than in that from apparently healthy individuals, although not exclusively. A New York pediatric hematologist was the first to suggest that the absence of sickled cells in newborns was related to the increased levels of fetal hemoglobin at that age.

It was at the end of that decade that Linus Pauling made his epic observation that hemoglobin from sickle cell anemia patients differed electrophoretically from normal hemoglobin, laying the groundwork for all subsequent work in the area. In the same report Pauling observed that hemoglobin from individuals with asymptomatic sickle cell trait appeared to be a mixture of normal and sickle hemoglobin. Two years later, in 1951, J.V. Neel concluded that sickle cell anemia was a recessive condition as defined by Mendel, such that both parents of an affected child might themselves be unaffected. These two observations form the basis of all newborn screening for sickle cell disease today, in which both the homozygous and heterozygous conditions are detected.

During the 1950s other abnormal hemoglobins were identified, and fetal hemoglobin was proven to be the protective agent in newborns with sickle cell disease, providing the window in which therapeutic interventions can be applied. But, most importantly for today's DNA diagnostic procedures, it was in that decade when V.M. Ingram observed, in 1956, that the sole difference in primary structure at the DNA level between sickle and normal hemoglobin was the substitution of a single amino, valine, for glutamic acid, now known to affect synthesis of the beta globin chain.

Despite the intense research into sickle cell disease, the remarkable observations first made in those studies, and the very high prevalence of the condition among defined population groups, testing for sickle cell disease lagged behind other conditions in newborn screening programs. Its role as standard-bearer was filled—and quite well at that—by phenylketonuria (PKU). It is noteworthy that the same laboratory which provided the means by which large population groups could be screened for PKU also provided the technical guidance for testing the same dried-blood specimens for sickle cell disease.

Cord Blood and Other Screening

Although testing of adults by use of electrophoresis was in use from the 1950s onward, newborn screening for sickle cell disease did not follow the path of PKU as an early component of newborn testing programs. Perhaps this is because it was felt that no effective treatment existed, but more likely it is due to technical problems presented by the high levels of fetal hemoglobin present in the newborn. Indeed, the value of early detection of sickle cell disease was recognized as early as 1961 by T.H.J. Huisman, who at that time began a study using cord-blood specimens to provide data on the natural history of the disease. A.R. Robinson had used cord blood for demonstration of his initial agar gel procedures in 1957, and reported evidence of HbC in a neonate. Shortly followed a report by V.J. Marden of the detection of sickle trait in a cord-blood specimen using Robinson's agar procedures and in quick succession other reports of the utility of cord blood and agar electrophoresis. In 1972 R.G. Huntsman published the "State-of-the-Art" in cord-blood testing methods and described the benefits of early testing. However, no mention was made of newborn PKU testing programs or the possible merger of the two systems.

Cord-blood screening programs using cellulose acetate and citrate agar electrophoresis were established in several hospitals to test newborn babies considered at risk for sickle cell disease, based primarily on race. These programs were effective in a limited population, but offered no possibility of widespread application in the way that dried-blood specimen (DBS) testing for PKU offered. That is not to say that the DBS had not been recognized for its utility in hemoglobin testing. K. Thielman reported in 1971 results of testing adult populations using a DBS and electrophoresis procedures. Although Thielman recognized the advantages of the DBS, no mention of newborn screening was made.

Solubility tests had been developed which could detect the presence of HbS in liquid samples, provided the level of HbF was not too great, thereby rendering it useless for newborn testing programs. However, solubility testing had the distinct disadvantage of failing to differentiate between the homozygous condition, sickle cell anemia, and the heterozygous, carrier condition. Moreover, it was specific for HbS, failing to recognize other potentially significant hemoglobinopathies, such as HbC or ß-thalassemia, or even HbS if present in concentrations less than 15 percent of the hemolysate. All these factors seemed to preclude testing of newborns using the DBS collected for PKU testing, until the publication by Garrick in 1973.

The Method of Garrick and Guthrie

Michael Garrick, while working as a research associate with Dr. Guthrie, applied his earlier interest in globin chain analysis to the development of a test which could utilize the newborn DBS to identify sickle hemoglobin. As recalled by Dr. Guthrie, Garrick's "research was devoted to the maturation of fetal hemoglobin to adult hemoglobin. However, my interest was to persuade him to develop a test for sickle cell disease to be used on the PKU specimen." Results of those studies were reported in the *New England Journal of Medicine* in 1973. The procedure relied on a new hemolyzing reagent to elute the hemoglobins from the DBS and micro techniques for their application to the cellulose acetate membrane for electrophoresis at an alkaline pH. In this same publication Garrick described a modification of the Robinson citrate agar electrophoresis procedure to allow confirmation of the initial cellulose acetate findings using the same DBS. This second observation has become important in current newborn screening programs, not only for sickle cell testing, but for all newborn screening tests: Only results confirmed on the original specimen by a second, different test methodology are deemed to be positive and reportable.

Although not reported in their 1973 manuscript, at that time Garrick also developed two isoelectric focusing (IEF) methods for hemoglobin analysis. But he preferred the cellulose acetate method because of the ready availability of commercial preparations, thereby facilitating its use by large numbers of newborn screening programs. It is noteworthy that this application of IEF technology to newborn screening hemoglobin testing presaged events 25 years later, an oft repeated characteristic of Dr. Guthrie's laboratory.

Garrick pointed out advantages for hemoglobin testing of using the DBS collected for PKU: use of an existing collection and reporting system, the applicability of this specimen type to large scale testing programs, and the difficulties of using liquid cord-blood samples. He and his co-authors went on to "...recommend that cellulose acetate electrophoresis of hemoglobins be used ... because five to ten times as many specimens can be handled as with other procedures...." Not surprisingly, this dependence on rapid throughput is the basic premise of newborn screening technologies for all testing purposes.

Current Newborn Screening Practices

As noted above, cord-blood programs had been testing newborns for sickle cell disease for many years, even before the introduction of DBS testing for PKU in the mid 1960s. Clinicians in Augusta, Georgia, had begun cord-blood screening in 1961 and, over the next 15 years, tested nearly 16,000 black newborns. Beginning at Yale-New Haven Hospital in 1972 for a targeted population 17 and followed closely at Cincinnati in 1974 for all newborns, rigorous cord-blood screening programs were made a part of routine medical care in those institutions. The advantages of early identification and diagnosis of infants with sickle cell disease were clearly outlined by investigators in these initial programs, and remain true today: improved and targeted medical care for the infant, leading to reduced morbidity and mortality; counseling and education of the parents regarding care for this infant and their risks in future pregnancies; and identification of other significant hemoglobinopathies, including alpha-thalassemia.

None of these early reports of cord-blood screening fully recognized the advantages of incorporating sickle cell testing into the
routine testing then in place for PKU. This was largely due to the
perception that the DBS was not a suitable specimen for hemoglobin testing. Regrettably, in his appraisal of the then-recent paper by
Garrick, H.A. Pearson focused his remarks (incorrectly) on results
from testing *all* newborns for hemoglobinopathies, rather than uti-
lizing a targeted approach as employed at Yale-New Haven Hospital. Perhaps this misinterpretation by a noted clinician discouraged
many newborn screening programs from adding testing for sickle
hemoglobin to their battery of tests. Numerous subsequent investigators reported improvements in the assays used for cord-blood
screening, but failed to address the central question of universal testing of all newborns for sickle hemoglobin.

At the time of the NIH Consensus Conference in 1986, four newborn screening programs in the U.S. were testing for sickle hemoglobins using the DBS. Louisiana had begun limited, target testing
in 1972; New York began universal testing of all newborns in 1975;
Arizona and Colorado added universal testing for hemoglobinopathies to their profiles in 1979. In 1964 Georgia had begun a program testing at-risk infants at six months of age, and progressed to
a cord-blood testing program by 1986, although still using a targeted
population approach. Thus the situation, as viewed by Doris Wethers
when she initiated planning in 1985 for the Consensus Conference on
newborn screening for hemoglobinopathies, was one in which only
a small fraction of infants nationwide were routinely tested for hemoglobinopathies. Targeted programs using cord blood were believed
to be the most cost effective and realistic, given the perceived disadvantages of the DBS. And, most importantly, a preliminary report
from NHLBI (National Heart Lung and Blood Institute) cited
overwhelming results of the efficacy of prophylactic use of penicillin
in lessening the morbidity and mortality of sickle cell disease in the
newborn. Thus the time was ripe for change—and that is what
ensued.

After two days of testimony and debate, the Consensus Conference recommended unequivocally that universal newborn screening for hemoglobinopathies be added as a part of all newborn screening programs. Importantly, the conference noted that current technology allowed detection of infants with significant hemoglobinopathies using the DBS already collected for PKU testing. Furthermore, the conference noted that testing was only the first part of a comprehensive program providing medical care, psychosocial support and genetic counseling to patients and families. With the impetus of funding provided by the Genetics Disease Branch of the Maternal and Child Health Bureau within the Health Resources and Services Administration, most newborn screening programs quickly added testing for sickle cell disease to their battery of tests. By 1990 Puerto Rico, the Virgin Islands and 41 states were testing for sickle cell disease. Among these testing programs, 36 test all infants and seven target "higher risk populations." CORN data for 1992 indicated that more that 2.8 million newborns were tested by newborn screening programs, with 2,940 infants identified with a significant hemoglobinopathy, 1,609 of these among the non-black population. These results dramatically illustrate the efficacy of newborn screening for hemoglobinopathies in the newborn period using the DBS, and emphatically demonstrate the futility of targeted programs.

The Future

The testing of newborns using the Guthrie spot as described by Garrick was only a preview of the utility of this specimen for investigations into hemoglobin detection and identification. The cellulose acetate/citrate system described by Garrick is technically superb, but also technically demanding and therefore was not routinely adopted by screening programs during the expansion of the late 1980s. During this time J. Black, apparently unaware of the earlier work by Garrick using IEF techniques, described a procedure using IEF on an eluate of the DBS. The technique offered simple setup, precast gels, clearer separation of hemoglobin bands, and later, options for automation. These were all clear advantages over the Garrick cellulose acetate method, although not without added expense. However, most states adding hemoglobinopathy testing during this period chose to use the IEF procedures, with citrate agar and/or HPLC as confirmatory procedures. High performance liquid chromatography (HPLC), long a stalwart in the research and clinical diagnostic laboratory, was chosen as the method of choice by California, the largest screening program in the United States. The automation and precision of HPLC were considered of paramount importance to that program, and its worth has been proven. Subsequently, refinements of the HPLC approach have been described, markedly lowering costs. Development of an immunologic procedure to identify individual variant hemoglobins has provided a final epitaph to the demise of the solubility tests. These immunologic tests employ monoclonal antibodies, simple procedures amenable to health clinic environments, instant and reproducible results with a permanent record, lack of interference from HbF, and moderate cost.

Among all the conditions presently part of newborn screening programs, sickle cell anemia most readily lends itself to molecular analysis. Not surprisingly, identification of the SS genotype from the Guthrie spot has been reported, using the tools of PCR and microextraction techniques. Subsequently, even the RNA of this species has been extracted from the Guthrie spot and identified. Incorporation of these molecular techniques into routine use in screening programs awaits technical improvements and simplification, and the concomitant reduction in costs. While no one presently expects these molecular techniques to replace analytical procedures for the native hemoglobin, their role in confirmatory testing, and identification of latent thalassemia syndromes is unquestioned. The author acknowledges with great appreciation the help of Michael Garrick in reviewing this manuscript.

Further details and bibliographical references for this article are available from the Wadsworth Center, New York State Department of Health, P.O. Box 509, Albany, NY 12201, tel: 518-473-1993

Awards Given to Bob Guthrie

May 23, 1962 Erie County Chapter, Association for Retarded Citizens
    Award for Science and Service

Dec. 8, 1962 Welfare League Plaque

Nov. 15, 1963 Education Service Award, Williamsville Schools

May 15, 1965 Willowbrook, NY

May 26, 1965 Olean, NY – Key to the City

May 26, 1965 Cattaragus County American Legion Award

1965 Advertising Women of Buffalo

Oct. 18, 1965 Kimble Methodology Award

May 26, 1970 American Association on
    Mental Deficiency Science Award

1972 Mill Middle School dedicated to R. Guthrie

1975 Exceptional Children's Foundation Award
    Los Angeles, CA

May 2, 1977 President's Committee on Mental Retardation Award

May 10, 1977 People, Inc.

1981 University of Auckland Department of
    Community Health

1982 American Academy on Mental Retardation
    – 5th Annual Career Research Scientist Award

1982 President's Committee on
    Mental Retardation Prevention Forum

Oct. 22, 1983 New York State Association for
    Retarded Children Award

1983 Association for Retarded Citizens
    – USA Distinguished Award

Oct. 1985 American Association on Mental Deficiency
    – Region 10 Townsend Award

Sept. 9, 1985 Governor's Citation

1983 Bethesda Lutheran Home – Pool of Bethesda Award

1984 Dean Stockton Kimball Award (from medical school)

June 21, 1985 March of Dimes, Buffalo and Erie County
1986 Kinsmen Club of Ft. Erie
Nov. 17, 1986 Joseph Kennedy International Award
1986 PKU Parents of Western New York
1987 Niagara County Association for Retarded Citizens
Rainbow Opportunities Award
Feb. 11, 1987 President's Committee on Mental Retardation
Oct. 22, 1987 Diocesan Council for Persons With Disabilities
1987 Chancellor's Medal
1988 Erie County Developmental Disabilities
Planning Council
Lions' Club of Milan, Italy
1990 The Robert Guthrie Award from the
Developmental Disabilities Prevention Program
1990 Weisman Award
Sept. 27, 1991 Biochemical Genetics Lab Dedicated to R. Guthrie
Sept. 27, 1991 Robert Guthrie Fellowship in Biochemical Genetics
Apr. 24, 1995 The Heritage Oak Foundation Founders' Award

Index

Bob and Margaret Guthrie surrounded by family members at their 50th wedding anniversary celebration.